AN ADVENTUROUS HONEYMOON

The First Motor Honeymoon Around Australia

Muriel Dorney

ETT IMPRINT
Exile Bay

Published by ETT Imprint, Exile Bay in 2026

First published in 1928 by John Dorney

ETT IMPRINT
PO Box R1906
Royal Exchange NSW 1225
Australia

ISBN 9781923205857 (paper)
ISBN 9781923527324 (ebook)

Cover: The Dorney's Whippet in Brisbane Street, Ipswich 1927 (Ipswich Genealogical Society).

Designed by Tom Thompson

Dedicated to those kindly folk of the outback, who, by their hospitality and assistance, did so much to make our trip a pleasure and success.

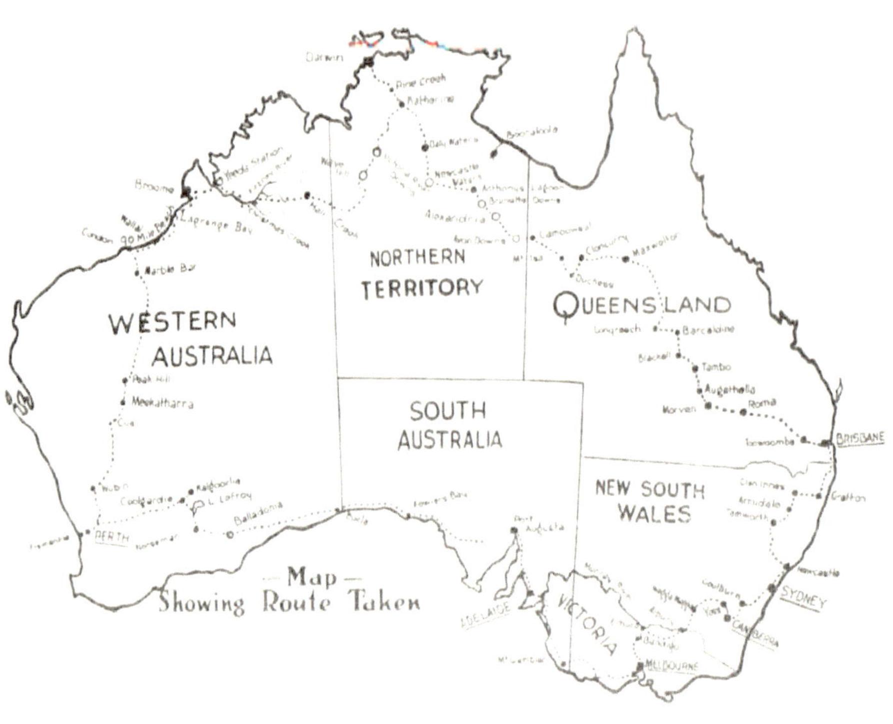

This is not a book of fiction, for in this story I endeavoured to tell the truth in every detail. If, however, in any matter I have been mistaken or misinformed, I pray that you will deal leniently with me, being assured that the error is unintentional. Until I took this trip I had no idea how little I knew about Australia, and, although I have never before done any writing, I am making this attempt in the hope that I may help some other Australians to realise what a wonderful country it is in which We live.

I wish to take this opportunity of thanking Mr. Bourne of Broome for his kind permission to use the photos on pages 152 & 153. On behalf of husband and myself I would also like to express our gratitude, not only to those hospitable folk in the outback, but also to those friends we made in the towns and cities, who went to so much trouble to make our trip enjoyable.

Muriel Dorney

"Leaving G.P.O. Brisbane."

CHAPTER ONE

WE Australians, I think, have had handed down to us a good deal of that roving instinct which prompted our forefathers to leave home and friends in order to seek adventures and wealth in a far-away land. Most of us, however, through lack of wealth and opportunity, are forced to stifle our natural desire to travel and see the world.

I must have received more than a fair share of this wanderlust, as from childhood, distant lands always held a glamour for me.

On leaving college I became a school teacher and, with that craving to roam still persistent, I saved what money I could, hoping that some day I might be able to realise my ambition.

A few years passed. Then came talk of a certain number of English and Australian teachers being interchanged. This seemed a wonderful opportunity for the fulfilment of my dreams, and a girl friend and I hastened to apply. Some little time later we were informed that the scheme was not being adopted by the Education Department, and all our castles in the air fell in ruins at our feet. Our hopes had led us far. We had even dared to hope that we might be able to arrange to teach for a while in such places as Canada, South Africa, and New Zealand.

I was teaching in a country district in Queensland at the time, so I was forced to settle back into my little groove and hope that opportunity would come my way.

Later I applied for a school in New Guinea, but a male teacher was wanted, so once again I was disappointed.

When, at last, I was transferred back to Brisbane — my

home town —I had quite decided that my chances of travelling were nil and, as most of us are forced to do, I determined to make the best of life as it was.

Then I made up my mind to buy a motor car with the money I had saved. After going through the necessary formalities—"When will I be able to have my car?" I asked the salesman. "Oh, you'll have to see Mr. Dorney about that!" was the reply. Thereupon I was taken over to Mr. Dorney, never dreaming what Fate had in store for me.

Several times later I had to see Mr. Dorney on matters connected with the car. Probably, however, we would never have become more than business acquaintances but for an accident which happened to my brother at that time. This brother was a photographer and, whilst taking a flashlight, the powder ignited prematurely burning all the skin off his face so that he was laid up at home in rather a dangerous condition for some weeks.

When this happened Mr. Dorney, who knew my brother well in the business world, developed the habit of dropping in every evening to see how the patient was progressing. I must confess, however, that Mr. Dorney spent more time with me than with my brother, so that by the time my brother was better Jack and I were firm friends. This friendship grew, and before long we were discussing plans for our wedding.

Then came the question, "Where shall we go for our honeymoon?" Jack was a keen motorist, and I had the motoring fever very badly, so of course it had to be a motor trip somewhere. But where? We thought of going to Adelaide and back, but were averse to the idea of travelling over the same country or almost the same country on both journeys. "Wouldn't it be lovely if we could go right around Australia?" said Jack. I thought it would be just wonderful, but it seemed impossible at first—just a dream—but gradually the idea grew until at last we found ourselves preparing for the journey.

For months before starting out we were busy collecting material for the trip. So many things had to be thought of and so many emergencies prepared for.

Our car was an ordinary stock model Overland Whippet. We

had the upholstery taken out of the back seat, the doors bolted up, and a flat deck built from the top of the front seat to the top of the back seat.

Part of this was on hinges, forming a lid, so that the back portion of the car was like a huge box, in which we could pack luggage and equipment. The lid had two secure locks so that we could leave the car anywhere and know that our goods could not be stolen. On the top of the deck we could carry heavy goods such as petrol or suit cases and at night, by placing various articles on the front seat to build it up to the level of the deck, we could make a very comfortable bed. Where we were out of the wet and safe from snakes, ants, centipedes, or anything equally unpleasant that happened to be prowling about.

As we would have to camp out so often we decided to get ourselves used to it from the very start and camp out all the way. We would have preferred to take a mattress or folding camp stretchers, but there were so many necessities that we had to forego such a luxury and we took just four blankets.

We carried a good supply of guns and ammunition. We each had a rifle and revolver and about a thousand rounds of ammunition in all. We thought we might need these for self-defence should we meet with hostile natives, and, should we get lost, have a breakdown, or get held up, we might have to live for some time on what we could shoot.

We carried a good stock of provisions, but these would not have lasted us long if we were dependent entirely on them. My husband had been for many years a bushman in Western Queensland, and he advised me to make calico bags in which to carry such articles as tea, sugar, salt, prunes, barley, rice, etc. It was a great idea, as the bags were so much easier to pack than tins would have been.

On the running board we carried a large â€œtucker boxâ€ containing all the enamel plates and cups, the cutlery and foodstuffs we were using at the timeâ€”our reserve store was in the back of the car.

Instead of saucepans we had a nest of billycans, as these took up less room and were lighter. We put these, together with a frying pan and two tin dishes, in a sack on the luggage carrier.

As we intended bringing back a record of our trip, we took with us a full-size moving picture camera and 5000 feet of film : also a good snapshot camera with which I took the photographs reproduced in this book.

We were sure to get bogged before getting through, so we took 75 yards of strong wire rope, and a winch which Jack fixed up to fit on the front dumb iron.

It was his own idea, but he is not in the least proud of it. It was sure, but slow—painfully slow.

As we were carrying two spare tyres we thought it would be a good idea to use all six tyres in sandy country, so Jack had four heavy iron plates made to fit on to each rear wheel, so that we could fit double tyres on the back as you sometimes see on trucks.

Above our petrol tank we had fitted a water tank to hold eight gallons and, in addition, we carried two water bags.

Of course we had a good deal of personal luggage, and there were very many other things we had to think of, such as a medicine chest, a spade, an axe and numerous gifts for the niggers.

A large kit of tools had to be taken, as we had to be prepared for all emergencies. Two small tent-flys completed our outfit.

A few days after we were married we left from the G.P.O., Brisbane, at three o'clock on Saturday, 2nd October, 1926. We arranged to leave from there, as so many friends wanted to wave a final good-bye to us.

I was not without my fears, but Jack was so confident and delighted at being actually on the track that I did not voice them, but just looked forward to the adventures ahead.

Many friends came out with us as far as Goodna to say a final - good-bye.

We had intended leaving Brisbane on the previous Saturday, but the car (which was one of the first shipment to arrive from America) was not ready, so we were forced to wait for a week. Although we chafed at the delay, it turned out that Fortune had been very kind to us because had we left on the previous Saturday, we would have met with very bad weather on the black soil plains of the Darling Downs. As it was the roads were just dry enough to travel on.

I nearly forgot to mention our dog—a large Airedale called "Laddie"—which had been given to us by a friend. We wanted a large, fierce dog to guard the car and to give us warning if niggers were prowling about.

Our goal for the first night was the Little Liverpool Range, between Brisbane and Toowoomba. We found a level patch there where we had tea and, as it was a beautiful starry night, we made our bed on the ground. Although we felt quite comfortable, it was hours before we could go to sleep, as everything was so strange, and we were so excited at being actually embarked on our big adventure.

We had not been asleep very long when we were awakened by Laddie's barking furiously. We got up quickly thinking of snakes and all kinds of things, but we could see nothing. Laddie seemed very nervous, so we came to the conclusion that, as he was a town dog and had never been in the country, he had probably been roused himself in a great fright by some harmless inhabitant of the bush.

Jack amongst the prickly-pear.

CHAPTER TWO

WE were up before the sun next morning, feeling just a wee bit stiff from our first camp on the ground, and spent some time rearranging our load. When we started off all the heavy things had been on the back of the car, with the result that the back springs were almost flat. We managed to bring the heavy things further forward and the car rode much better.

It was a very pretty climb up the Toll-Bar Range to Toowoomba, where we rose to a height of 2000 feet (approx.) above the sea and found ourselves on a large fertile plateau known as the Darling Downs. The black soil here is very fertile, and a considerable amount of wheat is produced in this district. The yield for 1925 was a little over a million bushels. Dairying is also carried on, and as we got further afield we found that this gave place to sheep farming and grazing. It was about lunch-time when we got to Toowoomba, so after a little lunch at a cafe, we continued on our way over the Downs.

Up to this time we had had our dog Laddie tied to the windscreen support by a piece of rope. He was sitting on top of a wide suitcase, but he was not contented with that. He would lean out in all directions, straining against the rope, and would climb as far as he could up the mudguard barking and whining in his excitement. He pulled about so much that he wore the rope through and, when we were going along at a good speed, the rope broke, and as Laddie at the time was leaning out as far as he could, he was spilled on the roadside, turning a number of somersaults before he could get to his feet. He didn't seem concerned, and hopped up to his place quite willingly again.

We decided then to teach him to ride without being tied on, but we had only gone a few yards when Laddie thought that he could just lean out as he had been doing before, and of course he came to grief again;

but he had learned his lesson and after that he crouched well back and kept his footing. The poor old dog had only one more mishap that day. He had ridden for about twenty miles without a "buster," and I do not know what caused him to fall off this time

We were travelling about thirty miles per hour when off he came again, and after skidding several yards on his chin, turned a series of somersaults. I stopped the car as quickly as I could and looked back expecting to see him almost dead, but he was racing for his life after the car and sprang straight up into his place again. He had worn some of the skin off his chin, and after that Laddie wasn't running any risks.

Indeed, so afraid was he of falling that for a few days, whenever we stopped the car, we had to lift him down. It was much better for him to ride without being tied on, and with all his tumbles he only grazed his chin a little.

For a whole day Laddie rode without a spill.

Then he saw some shorn sheep—the first sheep he had ever seen—and the temptation to give chase was so great that for the moment he forgot his many falls and just stepped off the car. but the somersaults he turned drove all thought of the sheep from his mind, and he quickly tried to catch us up.

After leaving Dalby we passed through miles and miles of dense prickly pear. This cactus which, by the way, was introduced into Queensland, is one of our greatest pests. Until the Prickly-Pear Land Commission took it in hand it was spreading at the rate of about a million acres per year over fine agricultural and grazing country. We are informed that now, by poisoning the pear and by the use of the cochineal insect, the spread had been stopped and the pear in many places is being eradicated. The poison used is arsenic pentoxide for young pear, and Roberts' poison (arsenic pentoxide and sulphuric acid) for the older and more firmly established growths. The thick, fleshy leaves are covered with clusters of fine, hair-like prickles which pierce your skin if you touch them, and cause a fester.

We were very careful when walking in among the prickly-pear, but I brushed against one clump without noticing it and it took me over an hour to extract the prickles. Even then some of the prickles were so minute that I couldn't see them, but I felt them and they caused my leg to fester in several places for some days afterwards.

The prickly pear is very popular with snakes, centipedes and such like, as it forms a very effective refuge.

They can glide in and out among the pear while men or animals cannot penetrate a yard into it unless a track is first cut. The track we were following was so narrow that the car would brush against the pear on either side. Laddie invented a game of snapping at nice juicy clumps as they flashed past, but, luckily for him. he did not succeed in seizing any.

It was among this Prickly-pear that we saw our first snake—a black one. We ran right over it with the car, then stopped quickly and got out, hoping that at least we had injured it, but there was no sign of it!

It had disappeared into the prickly-pear. I was driving at the time and Jack told me afterwards that if I had applied the brakes while passing over the snake and so dragged the wheels over it, instead of allowing them to roll, I would have killed it.

As soon as we pulled up that night we killed a large centipede, and a few minutes later saw its mate which managed to get away from us. A couple of large spiders hastily beat a retreat, and we saw also what we think was one of those venomous little red-backed spiders whose bite is often fatal. Ants were plentiful, especially "Greenheads," and it was just before pulling up that we had seen the snake I mentioned before. This was our third night out from Brisbane. The first two nights we had slept on the ground, but with so many crawling things about, we decided that it would be much wiser to sleep up in the car, so we made our bed there for the first time.

For the first few days we had fine weather, for which we were very thankful, because, although these black soil roads are splendid when dry, they are almost impassable when wet. One evening, just after leaving the town of Mitchell, it seemed as if our luck was about to change. Heavy clouds came up, forked lightning darted in every direction and the wind was so strong that every minute we feared the hood must be ripped off. We were in heavily-wooded country at the time, and owing to the danger of timber falling on us, we were racing to find an open space. Suddenly we discovered that Laddie was no longer on the car. How far back he had fallen off we had no idea, as we were so anxious to get a safe place that we had completely forgotten the dog, turned round and started to go back. Presently we saw two eyes glowing in the darkness and Laddie galloped up almost exhausted and out of breath. He must have had a very long run indeed.

All this time the storm had been increasing in fury and in a few minutes we were very lucky in finding a small open space. We drove the car into the middle, and with very great difficulty tied down a tarpaulin over the top of everything as we expected a tremendous downpour. We were no sooner settled than a great lull came and five minutes later the storm had passed and we had not received enough rain to wet the ground.

We were carrying two cushions with us to use as pillows, and during the morning of the day of the storm we noticed that the cushions had fallen out of the car.

I remembered having seen them a few minutes before so we went back to look for them and were lucky enough to find them within half a mile. While waiting for the storm to pass we noticed that one of the cushions was again missing, so after the storm was over we went back a little way, but the wind must have blown it some distance from the track, as we could not find it. That night Jack slept with the rag-bag as a pillow, and he decided to do that for the rest of the trip and so relieve ourselves of the responsibility of looking after an extra cushion. It was quite satisfactory at first, but as we used the rags on the car and for dish cloths, etc., the bag became so thin that we had to stuff it with our bathing costumes.

We were still going through prickly-pear country at intervals right out as far as Morven. One day near here we noticed that Laddie seemed to walk with difficulty, and on examining his feet we found that he had in them at least a dozen "bindi-eyes," which are a kind of burr. We extracted them and it gave him great relief. This was another instance of Laddie's in-experience of the bush, as Jack tells me that bush as Jack tells me that bush dogs can generally take out the "bindi-eyes" with their teeth.

There are many types of "bindi-eyes," but all are alike in the fact that once they stick to anything you have a great job in making them part company with it. I have spent hours picking them out of our blankets.

There was one kind in particular, like little balls of prickly fluff, which gave us an exceptional amount of trouble. When they touched anything they broke up into a number of little prickles, sharp at both ends, and many a time I have had to get up in the night and go hunting with my electric torch for the "bindi-eyes" that were annoying me. These that Laddie got in his feet were of a different variety. They were about half the size of a pea and had four very strong spikes sticking out at regular intervals, so that no matter how they were lying they were always resting on a triangle of three spikes with the other spike stuck up invitingly into the air. At times our tyres became full of them, but luckily the spikes were not long enough to do any harm. We found these and various other species of burrs in many parts of every State throughout Australia.

On the Black Soil Plains of Western Queensland.
(Note the absence of grass due to the drought)

CHAPTER THREE

AT Morven, 427 miles from Brisbane, we left the railway line and turned north to Augathella. We were now on open plains which, as a rule are covered with beautiful Mitchell grass. When we passed through, however, Western Queensland was suffering from one of the worst droughts in its history, and around here not a blade of grass was to be seen.

Soon after leaving Morven our "tucker box" fell off the car with a great crash, with the result that our thermos flask and all our eggs were broken. Were very sorry to lose the flask, as it saved us a great deal of time. I never drink tea, so at breakfast-time I used to fill the thermos with tea so that Jack, who has the true bushman's love for a cup of tea, could have some for dinner without our having to stop and boil the billy. Luckily, we were able to get another flask at Longreach.

We usually stopped before dark and had our tea, so that we could then drive on until we became too sleepy to go any further. We were well-equipped for travelling by night as we had two good spot-lights in addition to our headlights. About forty miles out of Morven we came upon some emus, so we stopped, and Laddie immediately gave chase, but as these large birds are such extremely fast runners, Laddie couldn't get within barking distance of them. We also used to enjoy watching Laddie chase goannas, of which we saw a fair number in Western Queensland. The goanna looks such a slow-moving creature, but is really possessed of remarkable speed. Laddie would be going his hardest after one when it would wheel suddenly and be up a tree before he could recover from the skid that he did in trying to stop. We were very sorry later on that we hadn't assisted with our guns and added those goanna skins to our collection, as we saw afterwards in Western Australia some tanned goanna skins that were really beautiful and would make splendid purses, bags, pocket wallets, etc., but after we knew that we saw very few goannas.

We camped about twenty miles the other side of Augathella, and next day passed, through the little town of Tambo. Here I tried to buy some meat, but the butcher informed me that they had nothing to kill and hadn't killed for weeks. We were to pass through many of these little towns later on, where the drought was so bad that there was hardly a hoof left in the neighbourhood, and the few stock that had survived were nothing but skin and bone.

Around Tambo we saw many mirages so vivid and realistic that, until we got within about twenty yards of one and it disappeared, we could hardly believe that it was not a sheet of water. Mirages are seen very frequently on the wide-open plains, and in many of the little towns we would even see mirages in the main streets.

From Tambo we pushed on through Blackall and Barcaldine, rising before daylight and driving until late at night, as we wanted to get into and away from Longreach before the week-end. We had to replenish our larder there, and had various other things to buy, so that we did not want to waste Saturday afternoon and Sunday in order to wait for the shops to open on Monday. There is a fine road between Barcaldine and Longreach, and we did the seventy miles in about two hours. The grass just here was beginning to shoot as there had been four inches of rain quite recently, but, sad to say, it was only local.

We arrived in Longreach mid-day on Friday, the 8th October, and left again mid-day on Saturday, after having bought all that we required. We had been experiencing some very hot weather, and had been anxious to know the temperature, so we bought a thermometer here. Although during summer a temperature of 120 degrees is common, we had difficulty in getting a thermometer that registered higher than 100 degrees.

Jack had spent many years of his life in Longreach, hut it was the first time that I had been there. I was very much surprised to find such a well laid-out town with such fine buildings, as I had expected to find a number of scattered tin houses.

There are practically no gardens in Longreach owing to the uncertain rainfall. The town never suffers from a shortage of water, however, as the water from a bore is laid on to the houses. This water, although clear, has an unpleasant taste, but it supplements the rain water supply, and as it can always be relied on, it is a wonderful boon to the town. It is also very handy for washing, etc., owing to the fact that it is very hot when it comes out of the tap. Most of the bores around here are hot, one being only 2 degrees short of boiling point. It is unfortunate that this bore water cannot be used for gardening owing to the mineral contained in it. For a few months it will cause everything to grow with exceptional vigour, but after that the ground becomes so impregnated with the mineral matters from the water that nothing will grow in it.

We were surprised at the number of goats we saw. All through Western Queensland and the Northern Territory we found many people relying on goats for their milk supply. I tasted goats' milk here for the first time and liked it very much. It is jokingly said that goats can live on the labels they chew off jam tins, and it almost seems as if it is true. They eat almost anything that grows and will do well where a sheep would die. Their flesh, too, is very welcome in the- cattle country as a change from continual beef, the flesh of the goat being quite equal to mutton.

From Longreach we went north through Muttaburra and Stamford. We were still travelling across black soil plains that were suffering badly from the drought. Only the stubble of the Mitchell grass was left, but we could imagine what a wonderful sight the plains, covered with waving grass, must be in a good season. This wonderful Mitchell grass, which is a natural grass, deserves further mention. It grows in tussocks to a height of about a foot or eighteen inches.

It is one of the finest feeds for stock and does not —like many other grasses—become rank when old. It gets dried by the sun, but even then the natural juices are so preserved that it has all the qualities of hay. Sheep and cattle can do well on what looks like completely dead grass.

We were hurrying through this part of the country as we had promised to be at Maxwelton, where Jack's father resided, by Monday, 11th October. The roads were very good and we drove late every night.

Kangaroos are very plentiful around here, and would often be so dazed by our lights that they would stand still in the middle of the road or spring across right in front of the car, and several times we only just avoided a collision with some of the poor creatures.

Within about fifty miles of Richmond we lost our way for the first time. It was fairly late at night, and at a fork in the roads we took what seemed to be the more important track, but after going several miles we came to a dead end at a fence. We had been following a fire plough track, so, as we were very tired, we decided to camp. We slept in the middle of the road near the fence, and the level fire plough track made a good bed.

I had never seen a fire plough track before, but Jack explained it to me. On these heavily grassed western plains when the grass dries up fires often start, and, swept on by the wind, travel at a great rate, doing very serious damage. These are caused in many ways. A traveller who is not a bushman may leave a fire without first making sure that it has been put out —a true bushman would not be guilty of such an act —and a wind might scatter embers into the grass or, perhaps, a cigarette carelessly tossed aside may start the conflagration.

But sometimes they happen without human intervention. In the summer out west dry thunderstorms often occur, when no rain falls, but vivid lightning strikes down and sets fire to the long, dry grass. The wind accompanying the storm carries on the flame, and in a few minutes a large bush fire is rushing onwards.

Jack tells me that he was once racing one in a motor car travelling at thirty miles an hour, and he only just managed to keep out of it.

Many cattle and sheep are burned to death in these terrible grass fires, the sheep particularly suffering great agony, as their wool catches alight and smoulders slowly.

In order to stay the fire in its course a fire plough-track is often made around each paddock. The fire plough is usually a V-shaped scraper something like a snow plough and is drawn by horses or a tractor.

It cuts off a few inches of the surface of the ground and lays it back on each side, leaving a perfectly bare track about twelve feet wide. When a fire occurs all the men from the neighbourhood rush to assist in putting it out. They set alight to the grass at the edge of the fire plough track and burn back towards the fire, thus making a space too wide for the flames to leap. As fire ploughs, in cutting off the top few inches of the ground, cut away the surface irregularities, they are often used in the country for making bush roads. This is what we thought had been done when we followed the fire plough track which ended at the fence.

At one station near here we saw a large number of sheep. As not a blade of grass 'was to be seen we wondered what kept them alive until we reached the homestead and were told that they were being fed by hand. Thirty thousand sheep were being fed at a cost of approximately £800 per week. This had been going on for some months before we got there and. I believe, continued for many months afterwards. Preparations for feeding were being made when we arrived so we stayed to watch the process.

A number of bags of corn were emptied on to a table-top motor lorry which was then driven around in and out among the sheep, while two men shovelled the corn out as fast as they could. The sheep picked the grain up off the bare ground, and it seemed to me that a great deal of it would be trampled into the dust and wasted, but the manager of the station said that he would be game to offer £1 for every grain of corn we could find after the sheep had finished feeding. The sheep were also fed with hay, because, as the manager explained, corn in itself was not sufficient.

A station man thinks twice before starting to feed his sheep for, after he has fed them for some time, he finds they have cost him so much that he cannot afford to stop. He keeps on and on. hoping for rain every day, and thus it often happens that by the time rain does come the sheep have cost him several times their value. We heard of one squatter out west who found at the end of the drought that his sheep had cost him £6 a head, whereas he could buy sheep for about £1.

Many squatters, having had experience in previous droughts, would not attempt to feed, but just let the sheep take their chances. Others sent their stock away, sometimes saving them, but in many cases finding that the drought became just as bad in the new pastures and the sheep became too weak to travel anywhere else.

Others again, when they found their sheep dying, killed them for the sake of their hides. This may sound rather cold blooded, but it is infinitely more merciful than allowing the poor creatures to die by inches.

Dead sheep were to be seen lying everywhere in these drought-stricken areas, and the few live ones we saw were so weak that they would fall down when they tried to run away and would not have the strength to get up again. Whenever this happened Jack would get out and lift the poor thing on to its feet. It would stagger away a few steps, but we knew that it would be only a short time before it would fall again and just lie waiting for death to come. There is one pathetic picture that haunts me still. Our dog broke away from us and chased a lamb about six months old, turning the poor little thing over on to its back. It lay there with its feet in the air, and when we picked it up it could only just stand. As we drove away I looked back and saw the poor little beggar standing just where we had left it, and it presented such a hopeless picture standing there with drooping head, for we realised that it had at most a few days left to live.

There is plenty of water in the back country owing to the numerous bores and network of bore drains, but of what use is that without a blade of grass? Even when rain does come it will mean the death of so many more as the ground becomes so boggy that the sheep in their weak condition have not the strength to pull themselves out of the bog and die where they stand.

It is a great satisfaction to think that, although Western Queensland is rather subject droughts, they are seldom as severe as this one. We passed through Richmond and just about dusk reached Maxwelton, where we had a couple of days rest with Jack's father.

While we were here Jack got a fly right inside his ear. After trying many things, we at last got it out by pouring peroxide into his ear. I mention this little incident because of its amusing sequel the following night.

The first Cloncurry-Mount Isa-Camooweal air service carried butter and ice to the inland in 1925.

CHAPTER FOUR

Right after leaving Maxwelton we camped on a treeless plain. We had got on the plain without realising that we were leaving the timber behind and so we were forced to have our tea without lighting a fire. Usually when we saw that we were approaching an open plain we would pick what wood we could find and carry it with us. but a couple of times we were caught unawares and had to manage a meal without a fire. The sky was overcast with heavy clouds, so we camped in the car, throwing the tarpaulin right over the top of everything. Just before we went to sleep a strong wind sprang up. and it began to blow a hurricane. I have never before known what wind was. The strong westerlies we get in Brisbane are gentle zephyrs compared with this one. However, the worst of it passed over in about half-an-hour. so we settled down to go to sleep, although it was still blowing in a good deal on my side of the car. I always slept on the side where the steering wheel was. as I am so much shorter than Jack. This night, however, on account of the wind, he insisted on changing places with me. About midnight Jack felt that he had something in his ear once again, and, still half asleep, started poking at it with his finger. At the same moment he moved slightly and put his foot on the horn. You can imagine with what a fright we both woke up, Jack, for the first few moments, thinking that the noise was in his ear and that he must have broken his ear-drum.

Next day, as we had no fresh meat and no chance of getting any before we got to Cloncurry. Jack shot a plain turkey. These are fairly large birds with rather long legs and neck and weigh about twenty pounds.

Some of their feathers much resemble those of the ordinary domestic turkey, hence their common name, although they are really bustards. We had seen a number of these, but had not killed any before as we had not been in need of them. They walk about on the ground, relying on their inconspicuous greyish brown colour to protect them, and, although they are strong fliers, only rise as a last resource. As usual we camped near a bore drain, it being the only available water in the country. I cooked the turkey in a billy-can and, as soon as possible, took some out to give to Laddie

He must have been hungry for we had had no meat to give him that morning, but he wouldn't look at that turkey. We had noticed before that he was rather fastidious, always refusing to eat raw meat, but thought that his "turning up his nose" at poultry was the limit.

We curried the turkey and quite enjoyed it, although it was a bit dry and tough owing to the drought.

As we got nearer to Cloncurry we noticed a great change in the type of country. It was rather arid and not nearly so good for pastoral purposes as the plains we had just passed over. The black soil plains gave place to red soil and rocky ridges, and instead of Mitchell grass we saw Spinifex. It was the first time that I had seen Spinifex, but it was by no means the last time for, later on, for hundreds of miles, we saw practically no other vegetation. Spinifex is very hardy and nearly always green. It grows in distinctly separated clumps, the leaves (if one can call them such) being like long slender straws with a needle-like point at the end of each.

Walking through Spinifex without a pair of leather-top boots is a very painful process. Even when green, Spinifex will burn with a great crackling like a series of small explosions. Cattle and sheep will eat Spinifex and seem to do well on it, but they will not touch it if there is grass about.

When we left Brisbane we had been unable to procure spare parts for our car, as it was just a new one on the market. A consignment of parts was expected in a few days' time, so the agents promised to send them on to us by train to Cloncurry. When we got there the parcel of parts had not arrived, so we just had to wait for it.

Cloncurry is chiefly a copper mining town, although silver and gold are also found there. There are several hills around Cloncurry which are composed of almost pure iron, but it is not worked, as coal is not found in the vicinity. This town has been suffering a good deal from the fact of its isolated position. We were told that all ore had to be sent some hundreds of miles away to be smelted, so that, owing to the expense of handling, only very rich ores could be mined at a profit. Now a Mackay Process Copper Treatment Plant has been erected in the town by the Mount Elliott Mining Company, and it is hoped that in future it will pay to work ore containing a much smaller percentage of copper.

Cloncurry is also a centre for a number of large sheep and cattle stations in the district. We were there a whole week before our expected parcel arrived. As it happened, we didn't have to use any of the spare parts for we had no breakages at all, but it would not have been safe to attempt such a long journey without being well prepared for emergencies.

Here in Cloncurry we saw a punkah for the first time. Punkahs vary in construction, but this one was a large rectangular framework of wood covered with cretonne and suspended by two cords from the ceiling. Hanging from it is a frill of cretonne about a foot deep.

A man sitting outside pulls a cord attached to the punkah, thus swaying it backwards and forwards, creating a gentle breeze. We saw many more punkahs like this one later on at a number of the stations where there was electricity and plenty of black labour.

When we were leaving the Queen's Hotel, where we had been staying, Mrs. Jackson (the proprietress, and the kindest of hostesses) loaded us up with things that she thought we might find handy on our journey.

Among these was a large block of ice. You will know how much we appreciated that ice when I tell you that the temperature was about 115 degrees every day. Mrs. Jackson also lent us her large thermos flask, which we took as far as Camooweal and left there with a friend to be sent back to her. Every morning we would fill both thermos flasks with chipped ice, then whenever we took a drink (which was about every quarter of an hour) we would add a little of the ice. How we treasured that ice! We kept it wrapped up in a tarpaulin and carried it for three days. Then the time arrived when we came to our last piece of butter and last piece of ice. It was mid-day lunch and I stood the ice on the butter, then turned round for a moment to get something else out of the tucker box. When I looked again Laddie was just licking the basin where the butter and ice had been. I couldn't say a nice thing to that dog for the rest of the day, as we could get no more ice before reaching Darwin, about twelve hundred miles away, and without ice we could not carry butter from Camooweal, even if it were procurable there.

From Cloncurry our route led us south through Duchess, another copper mining town. From a distance Duchess looked very pretty nestled at the foot of a range of mountains. A railway line is being built out from Duchess to Mount Isa. About twenty or thirty miles of the formation was completed and gangs of workmen were camped along the line.

Further out we found a number of creeks with plenty of lovely clear water, as it had rained there a few days previously. It was the first time since leaving Brisbane that we had seen any natural water worth speaking of. In many of the pools we saw little crabs, some several inches in length. It is wonderful how these little crabs survive a drought, as a few days before that creek had been perfectly dry and had probably been like that for months. It is wonderful, too, how frogs seem to spring up from nowhere at the first fall of rain.

Before the creeks dry up the frogs fill themselves with water until they can hold no more. Then they burrow down into the earth, their store of water keeping them alive until rain falls. This habit of the frogs is well known to the blacks, and when they are in need of water they dig in the beds of the creeks, catch the frogs, and consume the water, which they say is quite pure and fresh.

We had had no meat for a couple of days, so Jack shot a young kangaroo and we made some soup out of its tail and stewed a little of the meat. We made the soup by adding a soup powder to the broth and we enjoyed it very much. The meat, too, was very sweet and tender—much better than we expected to find it.

As we were nearing Mount Isa we met with the first happening to dampen our spirits—one which left us in a very melancholy mood for many days. Laddie had developed the bad habit of jumping off the car whenever we slowed down. We had been trying to cure him of it, but in vain. We were travelling slowly over a very rocky place when Laddie jumped off, but the surface was so uneven that he missed his footing and the back wheel of the car went over him. His back was injured, and he was in his death throes when we got to him, so Jack got my revolver out of the little cupboard under the dashboard (where we always carried it) and put him out of his misery. We had become so attached to him that it seemed almost as if we had lost a human member of the party.

At Mount Isa the surveyor, Mr. Gray, very kindly showed us over the mines, or rather over the proposed site of the mines, as Mount Isa will not be worked until the railway is built. To our inexperienced eyes the silver-lead deposits looked wonderfully rich and I believe, it is hoped that the place will be a second Broken Hill. Mount Isa is a series of hills in most of which silver-lead ore is found. The company is confining its operations to one hill at present, in which it is estimated there are from four to five millions tons of ore.

From Mount Isa to Camooweal, about 140 miles, was mostly a dry stage. We were told at Mount Isa that we would pass a couple of water holes, but that they contained dead cattle, and this we found to be true. We saw a plain turkey when we were nearing Camooweal, so Jack shot it and we took it into the town, thinking someone might be glad of it. They were very pleased to get it at the hotel, and we had roast turkey for tea.

I can't give myself any praise for cooking, because that turkey was fifty times nicer than the one I had cooked.

We made a habit of shooting turkeys and taking them along with us whenever we were nearing a town or homestead, and they were usually much appreciated. I shot a good number at different times. Jack would drive up so close to them that I was able to shoot them with my little .22 pea rifle.

Just before tea in Camooweal we discovered that our axe was

missing, and as it was a medium-sized one and we would have been unable to procure another like it in Camooweal, Jack went back for it. We had used it just a few miles out of the town to chop off the turkey's head. It had disappeared from that spot, but Jack saw the tracks of a man and horses. He followed the tracks for several miles and at last caught up to a drover and pack-horses and got the axe from him. He was just about to stick the axe into a tree and leave it, because a pack-horse man carries no more lumber than is necessary. It was strange that out there, where passers-by are so few and far between, he should have come along and seen the axe.

It was very hot in Camooweal —just on 120 degrees. Although there was no ice we were able to get a good, cool drink owing to the fine coolers they kept at the hotel. They consisted of shelves with hessian hanging all around which was kept saturated by water in a trough on top and at the bottom.

In Camooweal we received some letters from home. They had come by the aeroplane, which flies every week from Charleville through Longreach and Cloncurry to Camooweal and back. We were not to get any more letters until we reached Broome in Western Australia.

In Camooweal we felt we had been robbed when we had to pay 1/3 for a loaf of bread, and it wasn't good bread at that. Of course we expected things to be rather dear as the railway is over two hundred miles away and cartage is so expensive.

CHAPTER FIVE

WHEN we left Camooweal we felt that we had broken the last link that bound us to civilisation as we would meet with no other township for nearly 1000 miles, but we were really entering on one of the most interesting portions of our trip. A few miles from Camooweal we passed through the border fence (which is considered to be longest straight line of fence in the world) into the Northern Territory.

I had always pictured the Northern Territory as a kind of desert waste. How surprised I was to find such a beautiful country, much of it being fine black soil covered with Mitchell grass. All through the Territory we found black soil plains interspersed with patches of what they call "desert land." When I use the term "desert" do not conjure up a vision of barren stretches of shifting sand like the Sahara. This so-called "desert" is a firm red, sandy soil growing trees —rather stunted in size, it is true —and grass which is fair stock feed. I suppose it got its name because of the porous nature of the soil and no water being found there. This desert is rather more an advantage than otherwise, as it often exists in small patches and provides good shade for the stock in summer, when the heat is so intense on the treeless plains. The grass in the desert recovers very quickly with a small amount of rain, and so sometimes provides feed for the stock when there is none on the plains, whilst certain shrubs growing in the desert are eaten by the stock in a severe drought.

About fifty miles from Camooweal we came to the homestead of Avon Downs—a cattle station. Mr. and Mrs. Lloyd (the manager and his wife) greeted us and said that they had been waiting tea for about half an hour for us. We were surprised to hear this, as we had no idea that they even knew of our existence, but we found out they were connected by telephone with Camooweal and had heard over the wire that we had left at a certain time. We had been delayed, as Jack's coat had dropped out of the car and we had gone back to look for it—unsuccessfully, I might add. We were taken straight to the guest room, which had been prepared for us for the night, and we were invited to make ourselves at home. It was our first taste of that wonderful hospitality for which the Northern Territory is so noted and of which one cannot speak too highly. Everywhere throughout the Territory, and, in fact, through nearly all the outback, we were treated in the same wonderful manner. Although we were absolute strangers, there was the same beautiful spirit of brotherhood shown and we were always welcomed and made to feel at home.

Adjacent to "Avon Downs" is the station of "Alexandria. which is about 13,000 square miles in area, being exceeded in size only by Victoria River Downs, which is a few hundred square miles larger and is I believe, the largest station in the world. We entered Alexandria territory about one and a half miles from Avon Downs, and we travelled ninety miles that day before reaching the homestead.

Mid-way between Avon Downs and Alexandria we came to the Rankine River store —about the last thing one would expect to find away out here. This store is on the main stock route from the Northern Territory to Queensland, and so is patronised by the droving outfits that pass by. You can procure there almost anything you are likely to require —tinned goods, haberdashery, tinware, leather goods, crockery, and even drapery. Mr. Watson, the storekeeper, issues his own currency as money is very difficult to handle in the outback, where banks are so far distant. This currency is a cross between a bank note and a cheque signed by Mr. Watson himself and payable in Duchess or Cloncurry. These "cheque-notes" are circulated like bank-notes anywhere where the name of George Watson is known. Locally they are referred to as "shin-plasters."

Mr. Watson invited us to have dinner and we were only too pleased to accept his invitation, as there was such a strong wind blowing outside and not a stick of timber on the plain, so that it would have been decidedly unpleasant to try to prepare anything for ourselves. We had some "mutton" which was really goat, but was quite as nice as any mutton. People have to be self-supporting out here and most of them keep a flock of several hundred goats to provide meat, milk, and butter. Mr. Watson also has a tribe of niggers working for him, and these blacks, being fairly civilised, are handy for carting water and wood, looking after the herd of goats, and doing all sorts of odd jobs.

There is one other building here at Rankine River and that is the Police Station, where two Northern Territory police are stationed.

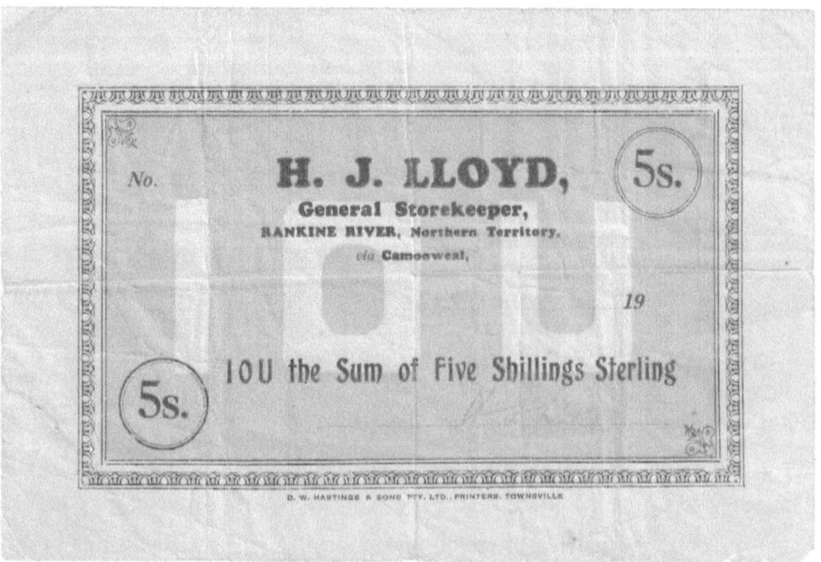

No.

H. J. LLOYD, 5s.

General Storekeeper,

RANKINE RIVER, Northern Territory,

via Camooweal,

19

IOU the Sum of Five Shillings Sterling

5s.

D. W. HASTINGS & SONS PTY. LTD., PRINTERS, TOWNSVILLE

From the Rankine River store we passed over the Rankine Plain, which was a black soil plain covered with Mitchell grass. It was thirty miles wide, and, if I remember rightly, we did not see a single tree.

At Alexandria we found Mr. Johnson (the manager) no exception to the rule of bush hospitality, and he made us feel at home at once. These large stations are almost like small villages. The homesteads themselves are wonderfully comfortable, and one often finds luxuries that surprise one, seeing how difficult it is to bring anything to these remote parts. Near the homestead there is usually a large store (often carrying several thousand pounds worth of stock) and numerous other buildings where are to be found a bookkeeper, carpenter, saddler, butcher and blacksmith, and at Moola Bulla (in Western Australia) we even found a saw-mill and a tannery with a tanner regularly employed there. Of course, all this only applies to the very large stations.

Good sub-artesian water is found all over the Barkly Tableland, mostly at a depth of from 200 to 300 feet, although we heard of a few instances of bores as deep as 600 feet. We had been travelling across the Barkly Tableland since somewhere near Camooweal, although the rise in elevation had been so gradual that we had not noticed it.

We stayed at Alexandria until after lunch the following day, when we left for Brunette Downs. Whilst few white ant hills in places; but here, between Alexandria and Brunette, we first saw them in very large numbers. The hills were not very large, probably averaging about three feet, but sometimes there would be about a hundred or more in an acre. We passed several bores on the way. These were sub-artesian bores and the water had to be pumped up by windmills. There is much contention about the word "sub-artesian." Out in the back country all water that does not rise to the surface is referred to as sub-artesian although. I believe, that any water which, when it is tapped, rises above its original level, is really artesian.

The water from many of the bores is only needed towards the end of the dry season when the natural waterholes have dried up. On some of the bores where a large supply of water is needed an engine is added to the windmill. At one such bore we found that a cow had died the day before right at the door of the engineer's hut. He was unable to get word to the station to procure help to move it and. when we arrived, the air was pretty thick. The engineer told us that he had been unable to eat anything that day on account of the smell, and that he intended walking into the station that evening, even if it meant slinging in his job. We were very sorry for the poor old chap, so Jack put a rope on to the car and towed that cow for about half a mile—down the hill, through the dry waterhole and up a hill on the other side. I will never forget that old fellow's gratitude, for it seemed as if he could not thank us enough for what we had done.

We arrived at Brunette Downs just in time for "smoko," as morning and afternoon tea are called in the bush. Mr. Cotton, the manager, made us welcome, and when he heard that we were carrying a movie camera and were desirous of getting pictures of the cattle work, he told us that he thought of having a round-up in a few days' time and invited us to remain for it. Needless to say, we were delighted to accept this kind invitation.

There were many blacks at Brunette and we enjoyed watching and studying them. At each station in the Northern Territory will be found a tribe of blacks. Some of the lubras, or gins (those are their own names for themselves) are employed about the homestead, while the boys (they are called boys, not matter how old they are) help with the cattle work. Under the supervision of white men they make wonderful stock-men, and their knowledge of the bush is a great help on these huge unfenced runs, for they seem to know every gully and rock on the place. It is almost impossible to lose a nigger in the bush, and their powers of tracking are marvellous. The blacks who work on the stations away outback receive food and clothing and an occasional stick of tobacco in payment for their services, yet they appear to be a very happy and care-free race. They are free to go and come as they please, and even the niggers who work on the stations go "wild" for a few months every year.

In the north only two seasons are spoken of—the "wet" and the ' dry.'" For about nine months practically no rain falls, then the wet season sets in and the rain comes down in torrents for about three months. The coming of the first rain is the sign for the nigger to go on the "walk-about," as he calls his reversion to his natural state. He chooses this time of the year (when white men like to be under a roof), as there will be plenty of water in the waterholes and game is so easy to track on the moist ground. Getting wet doesn't worry a blackfellow, as he discards such impediments as clothes before he starts out.

Not much preparation is needed for this holiday. He picks up his spears and boomerangs, calls his gin and piccaninnies (if he has any) and off they go. If there is anything to carry—that is the gin's job. A black-fellow would not lower his dignity by carrying anything but his spears and boomerangs. If there is a young piccaninny the gin has to carry it as well as her yam-stick for digging up yams—which are like potatoes. The water and what is left of yesterday's kangaroo (if they killed one and didn't eat it all) is also part of her burden. She has to collect the wood for the fires and cook the food—in fact, she is nothing more than a slave to her lord and master.

There is practically nothing that isn't on the menu of blackfellow. Kangaroo, wallaby, emu, 'possum, bandicoot, dingo, snake, goanna, mice, lizards, frogs, birds, grasshoppers, grubs and white ants are all relished. Of these the men hunt the larger animals, while the women and children keep the camp supplied with the smaller fry. The lubras also hunt for yams and berries and certain seeds which they grind up and make into a kind of rough cake. They are also very fond of "sugar-bags" as they call the honey of the wild bee, and they are adepts at discovering the tree in which a hive is hidden.

When on the "walk-about" the blacks usually travel in very small parties, as it is hard to obtain enough food to feed a large tribe. They never wander out of the country of the tribe to which they belong, or they would be immediately killed by the blacks inhabiting the other parts.

Brunette was a bachelor establishment. There was a white cook and a white waiter, and the other work of the house, such as sweeping, scrubbing, washing, etc., was done by some lubras who came up every day from the blacks' camp to do their various jobs. For their services they receive clothes (a frock being the only garment they wear), food and tobacco, and consider themselves a peg or two above the "wild-feller myall" who roams the bush and is not employed by the whites.

A white woman was such a strange sight to the lubras that I had great difficulty in getting near them. When, at last, I did corner one, she very alarmed and made funny noises that I couldn't make head or tail of. We had met some blacks at Alexandria and Avon Downs, and although I wasn't able to understand what they said, Jack could carry on quite a con-

conversation with them, as he had seen a lot of blacks in Western Queensland years ago, before they had been gathered up and put in the reserves in that State. The blacks always talk a peculiar kind of pidgin English and the whites, in talking to the blacks, do the same. If the white people did not do this they would not be understood. As we would be meeting lots of blacks for the next few thousand miles, I wanted to be able to talk to them and understand them, so for a while Jack and I practised talking pidgin English to each other, but my attempts at blackfellow talk were far from successful at first.

The day before we left Brunette an old gin, Larry, who had been missing from the station for a few weeks, came back. She was not a bit afraid of me. but came up and started to talk, and I was glad to find that —thanks to my bit of practice—l could understand a bit of what she said and make her understand me. Larry had been on the station some years before, when a manager and his wife had lived there. She said: "I bin member that one white feller missus long time," and, pointing to a younger gin, said: "That one Mary belongit me (her daughter) ; she bin workum longit that one white feller missus too."

We had heard a tale about the same Mary as we had happened to meet the ex-manager and his wife in Cloncurry. When they were out on the station an attempt had been made to train Mary to wait at table. She proved rather a difficult pupil, but they managed to train her to some sort of usefulness, until one day a visitor of great importance came to the station. The cook rose to the occasion and served a splendid dinner. Mary, full of importance, cleared away the soup plates without mishap. When the next course was finished the manager's wife said quietly to her: Mary, you bin takem meat." Mary lifted the roast off the dish, and with it clutched in her two hands marched proudly off.

Everyone was so busily engaged in conversation that only the hostess saw what had happened, but imagine the manager's surprise when, a few moments later, he noticed the empty dish in front of him. After that Mary was given up as a bad job.

As I looked at Mary I could just visualise the whole incident, but Larry awoke me from my reverie by asking me if I had a pair of scissors. I can't remember the word she used for scissors, and I couldn't spell it if I could remember it, but she made the action of cutting her hair by opening and closing two of her fingers so that I understood her. I confessed ownership, and Larry asked me: "You cuttem hair longa me?" I went to the car and got an old pair of scissors that we had in the tool box, and acted barber on Larry's hair. A few strokes of the scissors were sufficient to shear off her locks, as the lubras were not so clean that one would care to come into too close a contact with them. When the other gins saw what I was doing I had to act barber on them one after the other. The results were far from artistic, but as they had no mirrors I guess they wouldn't mind. In fact they were gurgling with delight and, anyway, it was a much neater job than they would have made of it themselves by hacking it off with sharp pieces of stone, or a piece of old iron, or an old pocket knife that a boy might happen to have.

We never saw a lubra with really long hair. When it grows a few inches it is cut off and carefully preserved, to be woven up into a belt or charm for a son-in-law, husband, or some other male relation. These hair belts are considered sacred and are supposed to have wonderful powers in keeping away evil spirits or "debil-debils" as the blackfellows call them.

We saw many blacks on the "walk-about" at different times wearing nothing but a hair belt and tassel made of human hair. They will trade almost anything for tobacco, beads or turkey red, but nothing will induce them to part with their hair belts. They would then be unprotected and the evil spirit would have them at their mercy, and that fate is the one any blackfellow desires least.

There were many little piccaninnies about, and I tried to get photos of them at their games, but the moment they set eyes on me they would open their mouths and yell and run to their mothers. They were used to the white men on the station, but were as frightened of a strange white woman as a little white child is of a black man.

Near the Brunette homestead is a fair-sized lagoon from which the water for household uses is drawn. When we arrived at the station it was near the end of the dry season, and the water in the lagoon was very low and very muddy. This, however, was soon remedied. As required, a tank full of water would be drawn off and the water cleared by adding a couple of packets of epsom salts or a few grains of Condy's crystals (permanganate of potash). This causes all the sediment to sink to the bottom, and within twenty-four hours leaves the water beautifully clear. As there was such a small amount of chemical added to a large volume of water, we found it impossible to detect the flavour.

While we were here Jack spent one day going around with the manager and some of the men pulling dead cows out of the bogs and waterholes. As some of the animals had been dead many days I am very glad that I was not one of the "pulling-out" party. The men all said they could smell those cows for days afterwards. It is a pretty unpleasant job. but is part of the game in the back country towards the end of the dry season, when the waterholes are almost dry and the cattle are weak. If it were not done before the wet season set in, the fresh water would be contaminated.

We used to enjoy the evenings at Brunette, sitting on the verandah and listening to tales of the bush. One tale which we heard about a kangaroo was very amusing. These animals can be tamed very easily and make great pets. On a station in Western Queensland there was one called Joey who was a great favourite. He was as tall as a man and as tame as a dog. Curiosity was his ruling passion, and he would immediately hop up and peer at anything he could not understand. A new jackeroo—a man just out from England—arrived at the station. A jackeroo is a sort of an apprentice working on the station chiefly to gain experience. He arrived after dark and didn't see Joey, but Joey caught a glimpse of him—enough, in fact, to whet his curiosity. The jackeroo retired to his bed on the ground floor and was soon lost in slumber. Some little time later the household was aroused by piercing yells. The jackeroo had awakened to find the kangaroo standing over him peering into his face. He had never seen such an alarming creature and he told the manager next day that those two big ears made him think it was "Old Nick" himself.

We were told that Brunette Downs has an area of 10.600 square miles and has 18 bores. These stations in the Territory are so large that no attempt is made to fence them. Brunette, I understand, has only about 200 miles of fencing. The homestead of these large stations is usually fenced in, and around or adjoining the homestead there is usually a horse paddock where are kept the horses for immediate use. Other paddocks may be fenced off according to requirements, but boundary fences are not erected. Of course, the stock from adjoining stations are liable to get mixed, but some of the stockmen from each nearby station attend every round-up and reclaim the roving stock. Young unbranded calves receive the brand of the cow they are following, and the cattle are drafted out into their correct mobs. There is some talk of sheep being put on the Barkly Tableland, and it certainly looks as if it should be wonderful sheep country, as it is very similar to the fine sheep country of Western Queensland. Before sheep could be put there many fences would have to be built, including dog-proof fences to keep out the dingoes. These dingoes or wild dogs do not do very much harm among cattle (although they often kill young calves), but they work great havoc among sheep and lambs, one dingo often killing dozens in one night for the sheer love of destruction, or just to obtain his favourite tit-bit—which varies in the case of different dogs. There are not very many dingoes in the Northern Territory now, but they would become a menace if sheep are introduced, as they are always so much worse in sheep country than in the cattle country. Several of the windmills on Brunette happened to break down while we were there and needed so much attention that Mr. Cotton was unable to put on that mustering camp when he had intended. We were unable to wait indefinitely so, much to our regret, we were forced to depart without seeing the camp.

We were four days at Brunette altogether, and then left about mid-day well stocked up with meat, bread, cake, etc., for our journey.

A Gunyah - the unpretentious dwelling of the Australian Aboriginal.

CHAPTER SIX

AFTER leaving Brunette Downs we found ourselves still travelling over black soil plains covered with Mitchell grass which here was in better condition than any we had seen previously on the journey. As before we would pass over small patches of the so-called "desert country" here and there.

Strange to say, since reaching, (near Camooweal) the Barkly Tableland we had seen practically no kangaroos or dingoes. Perhaps their numbers have been diminished by the blacks or maybe an extra severe drought within recent years has killed them off.

Just before sunset we stopped and had tea. The moment we stopped the car the flies descended on us in swarms. We had thought the flies bad at the homestead, but they were a hundred times worse here, probably owing to the better condition of the grass. We put on our fly veils with which we had armed ourselves at Longreach but we were continually having to turn out the flies that had managed to get inside. We were obliged to erect our mosquito net in order to have our tea in peace. A number of flies would get in when we crawled under but by slashing around with a cloth we managed to kill most of them. Tea without a mosquito net was out of the question as anything edible would immediately become a moving mass of flies. Whilst we were having our tea we listened to the buzz of the flies outside, and it seemed as if it would never stop. The last glow of the setting sun faded before peace and quiet reigned. What a blessing it is that flies disappear when the sun goes down. Usually, however, that is the signal for the mosquitoes to take up duty but we were lucky on that point as, owing to the absence of much surface water, there were very few mosquitoes.

Our net was made of dark green netting hanging down from all four sides of a rectangular piece of cloth 6 feet by 4 feet. Long tapes were sewn on to each corner of the rectangular top. To erect the net we tied two tapes on to the car and the other two on to trees or stakes or the shovel stuck into the ground. The net was high enough to allow us to sit up underneath it and there was enough loose net at the bottom to tuck in under our blankets on all sides so that we could sleep in comfort without having to fear snakes, centipedes, scorpions, etc. For this reason we used the net when there were no mosquitoes about. When we slept in the car we kept the hood up and tied the net to the inside back part of the hood and the two wind screen supports but when we slept in the car we only needed the net if we were troubled with mosquitoes.

Next morning we got up at the first faint suggestion of daylight thinking that we would have a few minutes before the flies started work, but we were hardly dressed before their annoying buzz could be heard and some were waiting ready to pounce on us when we came out from under the net. The buzz grew louder and louder as their numbers were reinforced, until there appeared to be even more than had attacked us on the previous day.

Preparing breakfast was a torment. Our fly veils protected our faces to a certain extent but the beastly flies swarmed over our arms and necks in a most aggravating manner. Jack, having had a good deal of previous experience with flies, was not much concerned about their walking over his arms, but to me it was almost as much of a torment as to have them on my face.

Three miles from our camping place we came to Anthony s Lagoon, which we had been told possessed the widest street in the world. There are two buildings there—a store and a Police Station—and they are about a mile apart, so I suppose that IS a fairly wide street.

We bought several things there and found the prices quite reasonable for that out of the way part of Australia, as all goods have to be brought either through Camooweal or from Booraloola on the Gulf about 150 miles away. As it was the end of the dry season the lagoon was very low but it is almost unknown for that lagoon to go completely dry.

Mr Walker outside the Police Station at Anthony's Lagoon.

We were told at the store that the policeman was away as he had taken two yellow piccaninies to Booraloola to be sent from there to Darwin to school. A yellow piccaninny is a half-caste child. Nearly all the half-caste children up there are illegitimate and the police take them from their black mothers and send them away to school so that they can be educated and trained in some useful trade. Half-caste women we have often heard referred to as yellow gins. We were disappointed at finding the constable away as we were told that he would help us to get some ribbon stone for which Anthony's Lagoon is famous.

This stone is very prettily marked with stripes of pink, grey, brown and white and polishes beautifully so that very pretty ornaments such as brooches, rings and sleeve links can be made from it. We found some at Mount Isa but it was so soft as to be practically worthless. The specimens found at Anthony's Lagoon, we are told, are only a little less hard than diamond and I myself have cut glass with them.

We found the black tracker at the Police Station and explained to him what we wanted and he sent several gins out looking for ribbon stone. We ourselves searched and found some specimens and, when later the gins came back with what they had found, we had a nice collection. We rewarded the gins with some tobacco and a red handkerchief each.

We paid a visit to a blacks' camp near here. There was an old chap there who called himself "Tilbury'. How he got the name I can't imagine. He was quite blind from a kind of blight caused by flies which always attack the eyes on account of the moisture there. We found this blindness (in many cases only temporary) very prevalent among the blacks. Flies do not appear to be any worry to a blackfellow. He is too lazy to brush them off and will walk about unconcernedly peering through a cluster of flies on each eye, so it is small wonder that they suffer so much from blindness. The other blacks in the camp were kind to the old blind fellow, feeding him and leading him about.

The blacks are great socialists and share everything. If one has a stick of tobacco he will share it with the others even if there is only a bite or a smoke each. This spirit probably accounts for the fact that the blacks, although a healthy race when roaming wild, seem to contract diseases when they become partly civilized and wear clothes. Even their clothes are passed from one to the other and so infection is spread.

We bought several spears from the blacks here and this is the only place where we actually gave money to them. Owing to the existence of the store nearby they understood that they could obtain articles by giving money although they had not the faintest idea of the value of it. Everything, to their mind, was a 'chillen.' Most of the blacks, even those on the stations do not know what money is and anyway would have no use for it as the nearest store might be hundreds of miles away. With food, clothing and tobacco they have ample for their needs. We found in some places where the blacks were paid a few shillings a week that many of them spent their money in buying drink or opium although it is against the law to sell either to an aboriginal.

From Avon Downs we had been travelling in a north westerly direction. Now, from Anthony's Lagoon, we went almost due west so as to strike the Overland Telegraph Line which runs from Adelaide to Darwin. With the exception of the monthly boat this telegraph line formed, for many years, the only link between Darwin and the rest of Australia.

From Anthony's Lagoon it is 180 miles to Newcastle Waters mostly over black soil plains. In some places, both before and after

Anthony's Lagoon, the ground was full of cracks caused by the earth's contracting in the intense heat of the dry season. Many of the holes were only a few feet apart and anything up to three feet long by five or six inches in width and several feet in depth. Progress was therefore very slow as, if a wheel were to go down one of those holes, we might do serious damage to the car.

Where there were no big holes the ground was often nothing but small cracks and lumps like waves of solid earth and bumping and jolting over these at any pace was fearfully uncomfortable and, in fact, made one feel quite sick. This kind of country is called "Bay of Biscay" country and, to me, it seems a very appropriate name for it.

A few miles out of Anthony's Lagoon we came to a couple of white men who, with the help of several blacks, were building an earth tank for a bore. When an earth tank is to be built a square the size required— usually with a side of from twenty to twenty-five yards —is marked out on the ground. On this line is built up a wall of earth about eight or ten feet high so that the surface of the ground forms the bottom of the tank.

Sometimes when these tanks are built they will not hold water at first. When that is the case sheep, cattle or goats are put into the tank while it is wet and their tramping about on the wet ground soon causes it to be watertight. This is called "puddling the tank." However, in some soils such as sand or limestone, it is impossible to make the ground hold water. Then cement tanks or iron tanks have to be built. These are much more expensive in the back country owing to the heavy cost of cartage.

We have heard and read many statements to the effect that the north of Australia is not fit for white people. When we arrived at that earth tank near Anthony's Lagoon the temperature was 115 degrees in the shade. One of the white men working in the sun (goodness knows what temperature it was there) without a shirt; not light work either as he was working a plough. We found that he was not even a native of the country but had come out from Ireland a few years previously.

In the north of Australia we met some of the finest hardiest men that you could find anywhere. Men of sixty will swing an axe or dig in the open in a temperature between 110 and 120 degrees and thrive on it. The white women, too, in the north, were far from looking jaded and aged with the heat as is generally supposed to be the case. We were on many occasions astounded to learn that a woman who did not look much more than thirty had children who were nearly that age. They get very little winter in the north and that little is not very welcome as most of the people told us they preferred the summer. The children, too, that we saw, were strong and healthy—far different from what we had always believed. Our experience of the Northern Territory was that, although it was very hot in the day-time, it was usually cool enough at night to allow us to sleep in comfort.

About the year 1922 the Government erected a chain of bores between Anthony's Lagoon and Newcastle Waters for the benefit of travelling stock. These are about twenty miles apart and, although the water of some is nicer than that of others, it is all drinkable. Each bore is equipped with a windmill, the water being pumped into an earth tank. This tank supplies a long trough, the amount of water in the trough being kept at a constant level by a float valve at one end. These bores form a valuable guide as the windmill can be seen miles away on the plain although sometimes the mirage plays tricks with it.

A Bore and an Earth Tank on the Barkly Tableland.

When we came to a bore with good drinking water (we could only judge by the taste) we would fill up our tank and waterbags so that we could carry on until we tame to good drinking water again. Some of the bore water is likely to give dysentery to people not accustomed to drinking it.

I omitted to say that at Burnette Downs we picked up enough petrol to take us to Darwin, a distance of approximately 800 miles. We would have been able to procure some at Katherine but we did not know that at the time. The petrol had been placed at Burnette Downs for us by the Vacuum Oil Company. We had instructed this Company, many months before our departure, to send supplies of petrol and oil to certain outback parts of the Northern Territory and Western Australia where supplies were unprocurable.

The little car was carrying a very heavy load with all this petrol as we had considered her overloaded before. We felt very sorry for her when we were bump over these black soil plains and fully expected to break some springs, but no! we were fortunate enough not to break a single leaf and arrived in Brisbane without having used the two spare leaves we had waited for in Cloncurry.

For the first hundred miles across from Anthony's Lagoon we went over an almost treeless plain. After that we began to find alternate patches of plain and desert. How we used to look forward to reaching that line of trees which marked the beginning of the desert for it meant a few miles of good firm smooth travelling, a few trees for shelter from the broiling sun and wood with which to kindle a fire.

One day we picked a nice shady spot in a patch of desert and prepared to have our dinner. We had everything spread out and were just about to start when we heard a rushing sound and saw a large whirlwind coming straight for Jack and I took to our heels and avoided the centre of it, which swept right across our car and scattered things in all directions. Much of our food was uneatable as it was covered with such a thick layer of dust and sand, and for days dirt seemed to be everywhere and into everything. We had seen many whirlwinds on the plains but it is easy to avoid them when you are travelling and none had happened to come right across our camp before. This one that struck our car was a big one the column of dust extending many hundreds of feet into the air.

At night we usually contrived to camp by a bore so that water for washing and bathing would be unlimited. In other parts where there were no bores we would try to camp near a well or a waterhole.

One of these stretches of plain across the Barkly Tableland was worse than the others. It was so rough that, although it was only about twelve miles wide, we took three hours to get across it and we were travelling all the time. If some of the people who grumble about the roads around the towns were to drive across that plain I am sure they would never grumble again but, of course, one does expect to find good roads in a town.

Near Newcastle Waters we passed under the Overland Telegraph Line, commonly spoken of as the O. T. Line. This was to be our guide right into Darwin.

We arrived at Newcastle Waters early one afternoon so decided to push on some distance before camping for the night. We could not very well lose our way as we had a rough track as well as the telegraph line for a guide and we were told that there were bores at intervals along the way.

It was nearly a hundred miles to Daly Waters the next telegraph station. Soon after leaving Newcastle Waters we went across another black soil plain similar to the very rough one we had crossed early that morning. When we started driving across the plain we could see the line of trees marking the desert stretch but it took us hours to reach it as we had to go as slowly as possible in first gear. As we had expected, the travelling improved when we reached the line of trees and it remained fair for very many miles. We had practically seen the last of the black soil plains for a while and from here on to Darwin the ground was of a firm sandy nature, sometimes with stony patches.

Owing to the sandy nature of the soil, an earth tank would be useless, so on this stretch the bores were equipped with large iron tanks.

We were fortunate to be travelling along a stock route or we would not have found much water on the way.

The flies were still very bad and we were having all our meals under the mosquito net. We were told that they were not nearly so bad as they would be after the wet season. If it is possible for them to be worse I hope I am never there to see them.

We camped that night about five miles past a bore thinking that the flies might not be so bad there as around the water. As darkness had fallen when we arrived there we were not troubled by flies whilst having our tea but there was a fairly large battalion waiting for us when we emerged next morning. We were kept awake during that night by the howling of dingoes. Their mournful howling in the dead of night is almost blood curdling. I felt glad that I had Jack with me and a couple of good guns. Although dingoes never attack human beings it is hard to believe it when you hear a couple howling close by in the middle of the night. It makes you think of wolves and feel glad that the Australian bush is free from man-eating animals. Jack switched on the spotlight and we saw two eyes glowing but they disappeared almost immediately and Jack could not have, the pleasure of making a target of them.

The honey of the wild bee would not be hard to procure around here as we saw a great number of bees. They are black, almost like flies, but a great deal smaller than the ordinary house fly, and have no sting at all. They crawled over us in large numbers and showed such a liking for a little water that we happened to put down, that we left them a good supply in a tin. I am afraid, however, that it wouldn't last very long as that day was the hottest we had experienced and that afternoon reached a temperature of 129 degrees in the shade in the car. We didn't find it so very oppressive, however, as it was such a dry heat.

CHAPTER SEVEN

WE arrived at Daly Waters late in the morning and were invited to remain for dinner. We were delighted to accept the invitation and get a brief respite from the flies as they are never so bad in a house as out in the open. There is very large homesteads at Daly Waters but only two white men Mr. Woodruff, the operator, and Mr. Grant, the linesman, lived there. Some years ago, before the automatic repeating was invented, a fairly large staff was kept at Daly Waters which was an important repeating station.

We were told that there was a large blacks' camp not very far away so, after dinner,-we drove over with Mr. Grant to have a look at them. He told us to drive quickly in order to get there before the blacks had a chance to clear out, but as we got near we could see black figures darting through the trees and going bush as quickly as they could. When we pulled up there were only a few of the older men left in the camp. The others we felt sure were watching from a safe distance ready to come back when we should go away.

This was the first wild tribe we had come in contact with. By "wild" I mean uncivilized and living practically as their ancestors had lived for hundreds of years. As Daly Waters is a telegraph station and not a cattle station, there is no work for them to do and consequently they are not supported by the station but just live on what they can catch.

The Australian aborigines are not beyond the stone age and they laboriously chip a piece of flint into shape for a stone axe and grind it smooth with other stones. They also make their spear heads of stone although we found some spears— the spear heads of which were chipped out of pieces of broken bottle or porcelain jars. Their fish spears have three prongs, each prong being barbed, and they are usually made of bone but we saw some where they had utilized pieces of fencing wire.

They make fire by rubbing two sticks together. A stick of hard wood is held upright in a hole in a piece of soft wood. Holding the upright stick lightly between the palms of their hands they twirl the stick rapidly by rubbing their hands together. This friction produces sparks where the hard and soft wood surfaces meet. With the aid of a few dead leaves or grass for tinder they have a fire in a very few minutes. Once they have a fire they endeavour to keep it alight and often carry a fire stick about when moving camp.

Although blackfellows are naturally indolent they take a great pride in their weapons and go to much trouble to decorate them. They cut longitudinal grooves in their boomerangs and most of their weapons are decorated with weird and strange designs either carved with sharp stones or painted with daubs of red ochre or stains from various berries or plants. We have brought home with us a shield that must have taken a blackfellow weeks of patient work as it is so wonderfully decorated with carved designs. It is made out of a solid piece of wood about three feet long, four inches wide, and from one to three inches thick, being thickest in the middle where a handle is carved out of the solid wood. A white man might just as well try to hide behind a blade of grass for shelter from spears or boomerangs as behind one of these shields; but a blackfellow will cheerfully stand up and let others make a target of him and easily ward off every weapon with a skilful twist of the shield.

The old chief at this camp near Daly Waters was quite friendly, probably owing to the presents of tobacco he had received from us. Mr. Grant explained that he wanted him to call some of his men together to show us how to throw spears and boomerangs. The old chief called out what sounded like several orders in his queer lingo and soon had a group of half-a-dozen men around him.

The way they can throw a boomerang is nothing short of marvellous. They give it a light flip that seems to have no force behind it and away it will sail spinning in the air for hundreds of yards. There are two types of boomerangs which can be distinguished by the different curve. One, the come-back boomerang, is used mostly for show, although it might sometimes be thrown in among a flock of birds when it will come back if it doesn't hit anything. The other, the straight throwing boomerang which does not come back, is the one that is the really useful missile and it is used for hunting. Long practice has made the blacks very accurate in throwing their boomerangs and their spears. You often see little piccaninnies who can only just toddle playing with tiny boomerangs.

The spears which are very long, some being about eight or ten feet, are thrown with a woomera. This is made from a flat piece of wood with a piece cut out of each side near the end to enable the thrower to get a firm grip of it. The other end tapers to a point. Fastened to this tapered end is a prong about half an inch long pointing back towards the broad end of the woomera. When the spear is thrown the thrower lets go the spear and, keeping firm hold of the woomera, continues the force of the throw forward with that. They can throw the spears about a hundred yards before they will fall to the ground. The woomeras of different tribes are slightly different in design but they all have the prong which fits into a cavity at the top of the spear and they are all retained in the hand after the spear is thrown.

Jack tried to throw the come-back boomerang and after several attempts succeeded in making it come back fairly well although, of course, his feat was very poor compared with that of a native.

The few gins who hadn't run away were hidden in the gunyahs or gundhies (called wurleys in Central Australia) which are their huts built of a few branches leaning against one another or against a tree and are so low that it is impossible to assume anything like an erect position inside.

When Jack threw his first boomerang it didn't come back to him but landed with a thud in the opening of a gunyah nearly knocking over a poor old gin. It was the chief's gunyah and gin but he didn't seem in the least perturbed and laughed louder than the others. I suppose he thought gins were plentiful and he could easily get another.

Jack also tried to throw the spears but met with no success whatever. They would usually go only about ten yards when they would hit the ground so, after breaking several spears, he gave it up as a bad job. The blacks were very amused whenever Jack would make a bad throw and laughed and jabbered away to one another like parrots.

There was only one old boy in the whole camp who possessed an article of clothing and that was an old pyjama coat one of the men at the telegraph station had given him. He proudly strutted about feeling very sorry for the poor old chaps whose sole garment was a loin cloth about the size of your hand and surely his heart must have nearly burst with pity for the younger members of the tribe who wore nothing at all. All except one of these, a lad whose name was "Ugly" had cleared out. Ugly who was about fourteen often hung around the telegraph station and so was not shy or afraid of the whites. The older blacks set him to work collecting and bringing back the spears and boomerangs that were thrown. Doubtless, Ugly is not cognisant of the meaning of his name or he would not, perhaps, accept it so complacently.

Mr. Grant pointed out a venerable old boy with a white beard and told us that he was the rainmaker. Each tribe has a rainmaker who is supposed to be able to cause storms whenever he likes—very convenient, no doubt— but the rainmaker usually has enough sense not to attempt to bring rain unless there are plenty of clouds about and a good chance of rain falling. If, however, he goes through the ritual and no rain is forthcoming, he does not for a moment think that his methods are ineffectual but says that some enemy with stronger magic is working against him.

One day, about a fortnight previous to our arrival, a bullock was being killed and the old rainmaker was hanging around the yard in the hope of getting some of the offal. It was a dull day after a long period of dry weather and Mr. Grant thought he would have a bit of a joke with the rainmaker so he said, "Billy, s'posin' you bin makeit rain, no rain bin come long time"? Billy, looking up into the sky and seeing plenty of clouds obligingly said, "Yowai (yes) Boss I bin makeit big fella storm." He went through the usual performances and that night, sure enough, a storm did come up. It was a veritable cyclone and blew with such force that it blew most of the roof off the homestead.

Billy had so much faith in his own powers that, when he saw the damage he had done, he went to the bush for a few days in order to escape the punishment that he thought would follow. When we arrived at Daly Waters part of the roof was still missing.

The Australian aborigine is very superstitious and a great believer in magic. Anything that he fails to understand he just puts down to magic. Each tribe has its magic men like the rainmaker and others who claim to be able to bring the kangaroos and turkeys and other game around in great numbers. They believe they can do great harm to an enemy by magic and have a practice that is called "Pointing the bone" or "Singing to death."

The man wishing to kill an enemy gets a bone a human one is often used for the purpose) and sings over it all the curses and evil things he can think of. After doing this for some time the bone is considered a magic one possessing power to do all the evil things that have been wished into it. The singer then points it in the direction of his enemy. The next step is to put the bone in among the doomed man's belongings so that he will find it and, finding it, know that someone has cast an evil spell over him and sung him to death. Once he finds such a bone he is so convinced that he will die that he gives up all hope and prepares for the end.

This custom has led to the development amongst them of the ability to lie down and die just whenever they like.

Across the chest and sometimes on the arms of most of the blacks we had seen were great ridges where ugly gashes had been. These were tribal marks and had been cut with stone knives when the blacks were young. The cuts were kept open by having dirt and hot ashes rubbed into them so that when they healed up they left great thick weals. Women also had these tribal marks but they did not seem to have as many as the men. Some such scars are caused by self-inflicted wounds which have been cut in times of mourning.

On the backs of some of the men we noticed terrible scars where they had been cut with stone knives in fights, it evidently being the object of the fighter to throw his arm over his enemy's shoulder and rip his back open. The old chief had a fearful scar from below his right ribs to the top of his left shoulder. The bones must have been laid bare and, had he been a white man, he would have had small chance of recovery.

We spent a couple of hours in the blacks' camp and then, after having given them a few more presents, we went back to the homestead to continue our journey. We refused the kind invitation of our hosts to remain for the night as we were beginning to fear that we might not get through the tropical country before the wet season set in. When they found that we were determined to go, they brought out and gave us some corned beef, bread and potatoes. Only those who have been in the back country can properly appreciate a gift of potatoes which, because they are perishable and so heavy, are difficult to transport and are therefore almost as rare as gold. We were very pleased to get some bread also, as for the past few days we had been living on a tin of dry biscuits we had brought with us and some tins of meat. We had, some time ago, been forced to throw away the remainder of the meat we had brought with us from Brunette, as meat goes bad very quickly in such a hot climate especially when it is wrapped up.

That afternoon, when we were driving along, we disturbed a tan coloured dingo having his afternoon nap in the grass. He stood up just a few yards in front of the car and then started to walk slowly away seeming to watch the car with great curiosity. He was joined a few yards further on by his mate. When we stopped he began to run but by this time Jack had got out his rifle which he always carried slung on the side of the car and in a few moments that dingo was kicking his last. Jack fired at the retreating figure of the bitch and, thinking she was hit, we followed her for some distance but she eventually got away and we could find no trace of her.

We came back and skinned the dog and that night when we camped we pegged the skin out. So hot and dry was the air that, by the time we were ready to move off next morning, the skin was dry enough to be rolled up and packed away.

One always takes a delight in shooting a dingo owing to the harm they do among sheep and calves. In many districts a price is paid for every dingo scalp brought in and I have heard of as much as five pounds each being given for them.

When a man has fenced his paddock with dog-proof netting it is useless until he has killed every dingo that happens to be fenced inside. Where dingoes are bad there are men who make their living by catching them. They trap, shoot, or poison them, and so wily are the dogs that killing them is a difficult task.

That day we had spent so much time in visiting the blacks' camp and in hunting and skinning the dingo that we drove on late into the night to make up for it.

Next morning we came to a creek called the Warlock about which we had been told at Daly Waters. We drove down to the right for two miles in order to visit the scene of the "Old Elsey Homestead" made famous by Mrs. Gunn's book "We of the Never Never." The Warlock which used to be permanent water now dries up for part of the year so the Elsey homestead has been moved down some miles to a more suitable spot and is called "The New Elsey." Just a few garden trees are left showing where the old homestead stood and a few hundred yards away the Maluka's grave stands lonely in the silent bush.

Soon after getting back on to the track again we came across a teamster and his assistant with two horse waggons taking provisions and goods out to Newcastle Waters. Supplies are only obtained at these outback stations once or at most twice every year. We were told at Daly Waters that we would be passing this teamster on the road and that he was "The Irish Mac" of *We of the Never Never*' . He was delighted to hear that we had read the book and we talked about it for some time. As is the custom in the back country they wanted us to wait while they boiled the billy but we declined as we were anxious to push on.

After leaving them we encountered several heavy patches of sand and later turned a few miles out of our course to visit Mataranka a station we had been told not to miss seeing on account of its wonderful springs.

Bird life about here was wonderfully prolific, gorgeously coloured parrots darting in and out among the trees. There were also galahs, cockatoos, finches, pigeons, quail and many birds I could not name.

We arrived at Mataranka just before mid-day lunch and Mr. and Mrs. Lowe made us feel so welcome that, although we knew we ought to hurry, we simply could not resist the temptation of taking half a day's rest and remaining with them until the morrow. Mrs. Lowe was the first white woman we had seen for about 600 miles.

Mataranka is a Government cattle station of 1000 square miles and has a series of most wonderful springs. There are many of them but one in particular took our fancy. A crystal stream of water comes out of the ground and, after flowing along for about twelve yards, disappears again under the ground only to emerge again some yards further on. The pool this spring makes is about five feet deep and about twelve feet wide with a beautiful sandy bottom and sheer sides. The day was very hot, the thermometer registering about 112 degrees and in a few minutes we were enjoying one of the best swims we have ever had. The water was delightful and they tell us that it remains at practically the same temperature all the year round and so feels quite warm in winter. It is good water to drink with just a slight mineral taste. In fact the water has somewhat the same taste as have the waters from the chain of bores across the Barkly Tableland which seems to suggest that the springs may come from the same source as the bore water. There was a decided current in the pool as the water was flowing all the time but it was not so strong as to be unpleasant. We calculated that the water would be completely changed once or twice every minute.

There were many such springs that kept appearing; and disappearing, but eventually they came up to the surface to stay and formed the beginning of the Roper River. There was one dark gloomy-looking round pool that was dark because of its great depth, although the water was so clear. No one had any idea how deep it was, but when anything which usually floats was pushed down a few feet it never came up again.

It was probably carried away down some of the subterranean passages, and if it could be traced perhaps it would be found to come up somewhere in the Roper River. That at any rate is the conjecture. There are no bores on Mataranka because they are unnecessary with such a wonderful supply of fresh water.

We left Mataranka after an early breakfast next day. Some miles further on, when driving on a flat open, stretch, we saw a strange beast that looked something like a bullock, but we recognised by its heavy build, its dirty brown colour and the backward slope of its horns that it was a wild buffalo. At Brunette we had heard many stories of the ferocity of these beasts, especially an old one like the one we saw near us. If they are alone it is because they are the older bulls that have been driven out of the herd by the younger ones. As a result their tempers are not too sweet, and it is best to give them a wide berth. We would have loved to secure the horns of this chap as a souvenir, but we had no chance, as even Jack's high-velocity rifle would probably only hurt it enough to make it savage. I held my breath until we were out of sight of that buffalo. Once, when it took a few quick steps towards us, my heart nearly stopped, but evidently the buffalo was only curious, as it stood still for a little while and watched us, then took another little run forward and stopped again.

There are thousands of these buffaloes roaming wild over the far northern part of the Territory. They are a kind of Indian Water Buffalo and were introduced from Java to Port Essington for domestic purposes, when an attempt was made to establish a settlement there in 1838. The settlement was abandoned after twelve years, and the buffaloes allowed to go wild.

From these the present large herds are descended. Buffalo shooting is now a very lucrative business, as the hides, which are about an inch thick, are worth from £2 to £2/10/ each. We are told that they are sliced into thin layers and that even kid shoes are made from them. A successful buffalo shooter sends away something like a thousand skins a year. Buffaloes are a great nuisance where there are fences, as they will walk through a fence with the greatest ease, even barbed wire having little effect on their thick hides.

About 11 o'clock we arrived at Maranboy, a very small settlement (I was going to say town, but half-a-dozen buildings can hardly be called that) where tin mining is carried on. Here we visited one of the Australian Inland Mission Hospitals where we found two of the most charming nurses you could meet. Enough cannot be said of the good work done by these wonderful institutions. They are supported by the Presbyterian Church, but are absolutely non-sectarian, their sole object being to benefit humanity and to make the burden of the pioneers a little lighter.

The hospitals are situated in isolated parts of the continent, where there is no doctor within hundreds of miles. The nurses are often called upon to nurse very difficult cases, and we heard of many wonderful recoveries due to their care and attention. At each hospital there are two fully-trained nurses who volunteer for a period of two years' service. What a wonderful sense of security the presence of one of these hospitals must give a woman out in the backblocks, especially a woman with a family, and how comforting it must be to know that skilled attention is within reach in case of sickness or accident! Another great work done by the hospitals is the distribution of literature. Reading matter is freely given out, and all that is asked of the recipient is that, having read the book or magazine, he should pass it on to someone else. The two sisters at Maranboy gave us morning tea, but we did not accept their invitation to stay to dinner, and pushed on towards Emungalen.

We had been all the time thinking of Katherine as our goal, but at Mataranka we learned that the railway line did not extend to Katherine where there was only a store, hotel and a police station. The important town was Emungalen, four miles away, and this town was the terminus of the railway line from Darwin. Until we got to Mataranka we had never even heard of Emungalen.

When we arrived at Katherine the police constable insisted on our staying at his bachelor's quarters for a few minutes to have a cup of afternoon tea. We then crossed the Katherine, which was the largest river we had crossed since leaving Brisbane. When I call it a large river I mean it would be such in the wet season. The water was only a few inches deep when we forded it, but the bed of the river is about two hundred yards wide, and it has very precipitous banks hundreds of feet high, and Constable Clapp informed us that in the wet season it often overflowed its banks.

The Overland Telegraph Line spans the river and the telegraph posts on each bank are set into great concrete pillars shaped like lighthouses to lift the line over the top of the flood.

We were now in the region of crocodiles, and were advised to keep a look-out near any waterholes or creeks as this river and all the others further north are infested with the man-eaters.

Emungalen proved to be a scattered collection of a few tin houses and shops, but, as it was only a temporary town, one could not expect more elaborate buildings. A big railway bridge was being built across the Katherine River—a step towards the fulfilment of the dream of a railway line across Australia from north to south. Construction work was being carried on to extend the line from Emungalen to Daly Waters, a distance of about two hundred miles, whilst in South Australia, I believe, the line is to be pushed north from Oodnadatta, but work is very slow, and it looks as though it will be very many years before the dream is realised.

The bridge across the Katherine was almost finished when we were there, so probably by now Emungalen has moved to the new town two miles away on the other side of the river. This new town is to be called Katherine.

At Katherine and Emungalen we were strongly advised by everyone we met to send our car up to Darwin by train, as there was really no road and the nature of the country made travelling very difficult. There used to be a road years ago, before the railway line was built but since the building of the line the road has been neglected. As the annual rainfall of from forty to sixty inches all falls in a few months, the road has become such a series of gullies and washouts that it is far worse than virgin country. All the people to whom we spoke thought we were mad to attempt the journey and did not hesitate to tell us what they thought of us as other tourists (almost without exception) took their advice and, leaving their cars at Emungalen, went down to Darwin by train. To make matters worse, there is only one land route in and out of Darwin, owing to the presence of tidal rivers near the coast, so that on leaving Darwin we would have to retrace our steps and come back to Emungalen again. But we had boasted before we set out that we were going to drive our Whippet around Australia and we weren't going to call on the railway or shipping people to help us, so there was nothing else for us to do but to face the journey. Long before we reached Darwin we were rather sorry we had made that boast as, but for that, we certainly would have railed the car back. But I am wandering too far ahead, so let me get back to my narrative.

Constable Clapp advised us to follow the telegraph line rather than the railway line as far as Pine Creek, as he had ridden up that way many times on horseback and knew the country well. He came out of the town for a mile with us to show us a very faint track through the trees that would lead us to the telegraph line, and then we could make that our guide. He advised us that if we saw anything like a fair track to treat it with suspicion as it would be sure to lead us astray. It would be a track leading out from some little siding on the railway line to a timber-getter's camp or some old tin or gold diggings or something of the kind.

A Few of the Old "Boys" at Daly Waters. At centre is the Magic Man who can produce rain at his own sweet will.

CHAPTER EIGHT

WE got about eight miles out from Emungalen that night when darkness came and we were forced to camp, for, if we had attempted to travel, we would probably either have broken the car or become hopelessly lost in a few minutes.

It was Guy Fawkes night, and although we had no fireworks the heavens gave us a display in the form of wonderful lightning. As on several other occasions we did not get a drop of rain. We had come so far without getting wet once or without having to go through a bit of mud. We were thinking how wonderful it would be if we could go right around Australia without getting bogged once, but were being a great deal too optimistic as future events proved.

I did some washing before turning in that night, and I must have used more water than I had intended, for next morning we found we had only enough water in the tank for breakfast. We were rather alarmed, as we were left with nothing but the water in one water-bag, the other having sprung a leak a few days before by swinging and rubbing against the mudguard.

When we discovered the state of our water supply we seriously thought of going back to the Katherine, but eight miles back over such rough country would have been such a trial, that we decided to risk it and go on as we would surely find a pool very soon in such hard rocky country.

The travelling was very difficult and slow. Sometimes we would be driving among grass which might hide a rock or tree stump, and to hit it would mean, perhaps, the end of our car and our trip. At other times we found ourselves among forests of saplings so close together that to drive between them was impossible, so Jack would choose those offering least resistance and drive over the top of them, pressing them down with the car.

Of creeks and rivers we found plenty— too many, in fact, for our comfort—but, alas! they were all dry! At each river or creek we would walk up and down the bank looking for the best place to cross and hoping to find a little pool of water. Wherever we saw an extra thick clump of foliage we would make for it in the hope that it was hiding a spring.

As the day wore on without our meeting with success Jack suggested that we dig for water in all the sandy river or creek beds we came to as water is often procured in that way. Many of the creek beds were sandy, but we dug several big holes and had as many disappointments. At last, however, our efforts were rewarded, and with delight we watched a little water slowly gather in the bottom of the hole. It was slightly discoloured, but tasted good, so we transferred several quarts of it to our tank. Then we drove on with much lighter hearts, but imagine our feelings when we found a running stream of beautiful clear water in the very next river we had to cross. The water was so much better than that which we had that we emptied the little hard-earned water out of our tank and filled it to the brim from the stream.

I was not driving at all between Katherine and Darwin. In the first place, Jack wouldn't trust me with the wheel, and anyway, it was the last thing in the world that I wanted to do. It was bad enough to have to sit in the car and expect every minute to be your last. There were so many rivers and creeks to be crossed and, although we always tried to find the best place to cross, the banks were so precipitous that I did not think it was possible for any car in the world to climb them. In addition, there were such terrible washouts in the banks with sand or enormous boulders scattered everywhere. Whenever we would mount one of these awful banks I would hold my breath, expecting the engine to stall and the car to fall backwards into the bed of the creek. Jack had more confidence in the car than I had, and indeed she deserved it, as our little Whippet never once failed us, and the way it climbed out of those awful gullies and creeks earned for her our life-long admiration.

We encountered so many river and creek crossings that I decided to count them coming back, and we found there were over ninety between Darwin and Katherine— a distance of a little over two hundred miles. Of course, we would often be crossing the same creek a number of times for the streams wind about so much in the hilly country.

As we had been unable to procure any fresh meat in Emungalen and were tired of tinned stuff, we decided to shoot some of the many pigeons flying about. That, we soon found, was easier said than done. We heard later that these pigeons are called "squatter" pigeons. They rest in the grass, and their colour is such an excellent camouflage that you can almost step on them without seeing them. Then they rise up with a whirr of wings from under your very nose and, before you can recover from your surprise, they disappear among the trees and bushes. We chased those pigeons for about an hour and then found ourselves the possessors of one solitary bird. We seriously wondered whether it was worth-while going to the trouble of making a stew of just one pigeon, but it was such a plump little bird and we were so starving for a taste of fresh meat, that we decided to cook it. When we camped that night I gathered wood for a fire while Jack cleaned the pigeon. We eked that little bird out with a lot of bread and and made a most enjoyable meal of it.

That calls to mind how Jack used to tease me about the fires I made. He nearly always made the fires, and would build a big one—nearly fit to roast an ox. Then he would pile wood on and wait for it burn down, the result being a glowing bed of coals so hot that when I attempted to do toast or fry anything I would cook myself almost as much as the food. When I made a fire I would make a nice little one a few inches in diameter, just big enough for the thing I was cooking.

It used to burn down very quickly, I know, but I always had a pile of chips handy and kept feeding it. Jack used to call it a blackfellow's fire, for it seems that when a blackfellow wants to warm himself he sits down on the ground and makes a little fire between his legs, then wraps himself right around it. He keeps feeding it from a pile of stick as I did, so I suppose Jack was quite justified in teasing me. Anyway, we compromised and I built the fires a little larger so that they wouldn't burn out so quickly and Jack reduced the size of his.

Where possible we always camped in an open space, so that trees or limbs would not fall on us during the night. An open camp, however, was not so nice when morning came, and the burning rays of the sun shone on us while we were trying to get a bit of breakfast. We didn't trouble to erect the fly every night, as it wasted too much time, so we used to get up before daylight every morning and try to get our breakfast over before the sun got too high.

Next morning, we had not travelled very far, when we came to the little township of Pine Creek. This place was once far more important than it is now for, some years ago, a good deal of gold was found around there. As it was Sunday we were unable to get any fresh meat, but we managed to buy some bread.

Most of our travelling from Katherine had been so rough and slow that we had been forced to use first or second gear nearly all the time. This was using up so much of our petrol that we were afraid we would not have enough to see us through to Darwin. We had, therefore, to procure some in Pine Creek, that being the only settlement of any size before reaching Darwin.

We made many inquiries and were almost beginning to despair of getting any, and were dreading the possibility of a long walk into Darwin if our petrol gave out, when we managed to get one tin. After all our trouble, however, we did not have to use that tin of petrol.

From Pine Creek the railway and telegraph lines run close together practically all the way. About every ten or twelve miles along the railway line we would come to a deserted cottage or sometimes two of them together.

Some years ago the lengthsmen who looked after the line lived in these little cottages. They used to travel to and from their work on hand-driven trolleys and, as they could not travel far in that manner, lengthsmen were stationed every few miles along the line. Now motor trolleys are used to take the lengthsmen about, and, as they can cover such a lot of ground, a much smaller number of men look after the line, so the cottages have been deserted.

In Pine Creek we were informed that the rest of our journey to Darwin would be worse than the part we had traversed from Katherine, and we had not gone far on our way before we believed it. We had been warned against the journey by car, but in our most pessimistic moments we had not imagined anything approaching what the trip turned out to be.

We were driving along in grass about a foot high when, without warning, we felt a terrible jar which brought the car to a dead stop. Luckily, we were travelling very slowly (it was impossible to do anything else), or I do not know what would have happened. Anxiously we got out to see the damage done, and I would not have been surprised to find that our car was undriveable. However, we were delighted to find that nothing was broken—not even a spring—but the front axle was pretty badly bent. We had flopped into two large holes so placed that the front wheels fell into them simultaneously. The rest of this incident—although perfectly true—seems almost like a fairy story, so greatly did Fortune favour us.

Within sight, only a couple of hundred yards away, was one of those deserted cottages to which I have referred. We could see a shed near this one and, in the hope of finding something that might be of use to us, we went over to it. Here we found a jim-crow, and when Jack saw it his delight knew no bounds, although, until he explained it to me, I couldn't see what there was in that queer-looking thing to make him go into such ecstasies. A jim-crow, he explained to me, is a device used for bending rails. It is a U-shaped affair with a hook at each end. Up the centre of the U's a long, strong screw which is tightened by means of a lever. The hooks at each end of the U are placed over the rail to grip it; then, as the screw in the centre is screwed up, it forces the middle of the rail away, thus bending it.

It was made of heavy iron, but Jack carried it over to the car and we found to our delight that it fitted the axle exactly. A couple of turns of the screw and our axle was straight. For several days we could talk of nothing but our wonderful luck.

That afternoon we actually found ourselves driving along a bit of a track for a while. We were beginning to suspect that it was leading us astray when we came upon a small cultivation and some mean-looking huts. Just ahead of us on the track was a Chinaman.

He evidently didn't hear us, for he jumped aside in a great fright when we tooted our horn and stood smiling and bowing to us. We stopped and asked him if that was the right road to Brock's Creek, which we had been told was the next place on the railway line. With much waving of arms he broke into a chant which sounded something like this:

We, of course, came to the conclusion that the poor old chap couldn't speak a word of English so, thanking him with nods, we drove on towards the huts.

Here we found several more Chinamen who replied to our queries in the same manner, although they weren't quite so musical about it. There was nothing for it but to keep on, and we were delighted to find that the track turned and went east again and, after a few miles, we were relieved to catch sight of the railway line once more.

At Brock's Creek there is an old deserted gold mine. The caretaker of the plant (the only white man living there) was away from home and we could not get any satisfactory information from the few blacks we met.

When we asked the most intelligent-looking boy how far Adelaide River was, he said: "Mile un a bit." Jack said it reminded him of a joke he once heard.

A white man asked a blackfellow how far it was to a certain place: "Oh, bout mile un a bit" was the reply- How far is the bit?" said the white man. " 'Bout nine mile, said the blackfellow. In our case the bit proved to be even more than that. It is peculiar how the blacks do not seem to be able to grasp any idea of the white man's measurements. They judge distance by how long it would take them to walk to a place, and will tell you where the sun will be when they get there.

As not at lightened by the black-fellow's information we just continued on our way and, when the sun was getting near the horizon, we came to a deserted cottage at which we decided to spend the night.

These deserted cottages consist of two rooms with a verandah back and front. They are built of galvanised iron and the floors of both rooms and verandahs are made of cement, so that no part of the house can be attacked by white ants. could not get inside this house, as the doors and windows were bolted, but we made a very comfortable camp on the verandah. The cement, being so level, formed a much more comfortable bed than the stony ground on which we had slept the last few nights. The tank here was still in good condition, and half full of lovely rain water, so we had no need to stint ourselves in that direction.

Luck was with us once again in our having a roof over our heads on that particular night, as towards morning a sharp shower fell which would have been very troublesome if we had been sleeping on the ground without a cover.

Next morning we saw our second snake, and a beauty it was, too. It was of a greenish black colour on the back and yellowish green underneath, and it must have been at least twelve feet long. Jack quickly got his gun out. as shooting would be the easiest way of killing it. By the time Jack had his gun ready it had disappeared among some undergrowth, and we were unable to catch sight of it again. We were told in Darwin that it was probably a rock python, as there are many of them about those parts and they grow to a length of from fifteen to twenty feet.

Once that day we roamed a long way out of our course. We should have remembered the warning we had received in Katherine about not following anything that looked like a good track, but the formation of the land was such that any other course seemed impossible, and so we kept on and on, although the position of the sun told us that we were going in the wrong direction.

About seven miles from where we had lost sight of the line we came to a Chinese garden and banana farm, the owner of which could talk a little broken English. He told us that was the end of the road, but he could not give us any information about how to get to Darwin. for, of course, he always went by train from a small siding. So we doubled back on our tracks, and on reaching the railway line again we searched until we found a passage in between two large masses of rock where, by going over a forest of young saplings, we were able to make progress in the right direction. In pushing down these saplings we broke our lamp stay rod (the small bar connecting the two headlamps), but that was of minor importance, and Jack easily made a new one in Darwin.

That day we saw a very fine bower-bird's playground, and as Jack said it was an extremely good specimen I took a photograph of it. We did not see the birds, as they must have flown off at our approach but we knew by the number of fresh green berries in it that the playground was still in use. The birds build these playgrounds for amusement, using them as a place to play about in, and there they hoard up objects that take their fancy. This one contained a large number of white bleached snail shells and berries. If the play-ground was built anywhere near civilisation it would probably contain pieces of broken glass, tin, china, or, in fact, anything bright that the birds could get hold of. Lost jewellery, spoons, trinkets, etc., have often been found in a bower-bird's playground.

Many times during the last few days we had to retrace our steps for some distance, as we have to retrace our steps for some distance, as we would find an uncrossable creek or gully or enormous boulders blocking our path. In some places we could see traces of the old road, but mostly those were places to be avoided owing to the numerous washouts which were several feet deep in places.

In many parts we found pandanus palms which usually grow in swampy country. At this time of the year however, the swamps had completely dried up and the ground was so fearfully rough and lumpy that driving over it was torture, even although we went as slowly as possible in low gear. We frequently heard this kind of ground referred to outback as "debil-debil country," and it bears a close resemblance to the "Bay country" we passed over on the Barkly Tableland.

At intervals throughout the whole trip we had seen ant-hills, and the further north we went the larger we found them. Four different times I had taken photos of what we thought was the biggest one we would find and here now we found ant-hills that eclipsed all the others. We saw many by the telegraph line and they were higher than the telegraph poles which, by the way, are made of iron to resist the raids of these termites. Some of the hills were about twenty feet in height and of enormous bulk, often bearing a quaint resemblance to an old world with its numerous turrets. We noticed they are always built in sandy soil and we are told they are made of the soil mixed with the saliva of the insect. We broke some open with the axe and found a network of passages filled with white ants, eggs, and a large amount of little pieces of grass stalks from a quarter to half an inch long. Evidently, besides being a home, the ant-hill is a store-house where food is laid by for the wet season where there will perhaps be several inches of water on the ground, so that no ant can go abroad.

In some hills we found the ants were very small and of a reddish tinge, while in other hills they were practically the same as the white ant we have in Queensland only a great deal larger, being half or even three-quarters of an inch in length.

Although white ants will eat almost anything their chief food is wood. They will eat all the inside out of a log so that it becomes a mere shell through which you can poke your finger. In a tropical climate where these termites abound they are one of the worst pests. They attack houses if they are built of wood, and that is one of the reasons why we found in the outback so many galvanised iron houses with floors of cement. Another reason why galvanised iron is used so extensively is because it is so easily transported and erected. Where wooden houses are built a protecting cap or iron is placed between the stump and the building to keep out the white ants. Stumps are sometimes built on bricks or cement or one of the few kinds of wood that the ants will not attack.

We found later on that white ants are so bad in Darwin that they even attack garden plants, vegetables and many ornamental trees. The first process in making a garden there is to cover your yard with cement, then stand oil drums, petrol tins, barrels, or such like, on the cement, and make your garden in these. One lady told us that when a crack appeared in the cement the ants came up through the crack. After that she took the precaution of standing all her tins on bricks.

Although the white ant is such a pest, it is one that should not be difficult to eradicate if it were seriously taken in hand, owing to its peculiar habits. It is a cannibal and will eat its dead companions, but, still more strange, when food has once passed through its body it will re-eat it and re-eat it again until there is not a particle of nourishment left in it. When dealing with white ants, therefore, a little poison has far reaching effects. If a few ants are poisoned they are immediately eaten by their comrades who die and are eaten by others, and so on until the whole community is exterminated. The breaking up of the ground is harmful to white ants which are helpless insects and like to live and work in the dark.

While talking of white ants, I must tell you about some queer white ant hills we saw when close to Darwin. They were flat slab-like structures (not as tail as the others). being anything up to ten feet in height and four or five feet in width. They are not very thick through, usually about a foot or eighteen inches at the bottom and tapering to a knife edge at the top. A group of several hundred on one flat bore a very eerie resemblance to a cemetery, as all the slabs were facing the same way. We learned later that these were built by a particular kind of termite called the meridian ant, and the hills are called magnetic ant-hills because of the fact that they always point north and south. by this I mean that the thin ends of the slabs form the northern and southern extremities, while the flat surfaces are exposed to the east and west. On our return journey to Katherine we tested the truth of this with our compass and although we found the hills both isolated and in groups we could not find one that was not pointing north and south. We could get no explanation as to the cause of this phenomenon.

The white ant-hills are made some use of in the north. Broken up and rolled they make splendid tennis courts. When crumbled and moistened very enduring pise houses can be built of them, and we even saw bakers' ovens made of the same material but to get back to our story.

Towards mid-day we came to a large pool of water which (although we did not know it at the time) was part of the Darwin River. It was a very pretty sight with its heavily wooded banks and patches of water-lilies. Swimming about were several wild ducks of that species called pigmy geese. The sight of these made our mouths water, so we crept along the bank with my little .22 rifle (as we did not possess a shot gun), and very soon four dead ducks lay floating on the surface of the water. Now, how to get them out was the problem. Everything looked so calm and peaceful that Jack would have gone in after them, but for my vehement protests. Only that morning we had seen near a siding a large dead crocodile over ten feet long which had been poisoned by a man because it had come out of the water and killed one of his bullocks and mangled another.

Finally we had to resort to very primitive methods to get those ducks out of the water. We tied a small but very heavy branch to the end of a long piece of rope. Then Jack threw that branch out until he happened to throw it right over a duck, so that by hauling in the branch we pulled the duck to shore. After many futile attempts, owing to the width of the stream, we had to content ourselves with two of the four ducks. Having plenty of water handy, we crawled out on to a big long and cleaned them. It was a case of "Ignorance is °Bliss" as we were told afterwards by an old hand who knew the country well that the pool was so infested with crocodiles that he wouldn't dare to dip a billy of water out of it unless he had the billy tied to a long stick. It seems that crocodiles lie in wait just below the surface ready to seize the first unsuspecting animal or person who wanders near. The crocodile likes his meat ripe, so that he does not eat his prey at once, but buries it under a log or in some nook at the bottom of a river for several days. We were told that the reason for this was that the crocodile had no grinding teeth and only a small swallow, so that it had to let its meat putrify in order to tear it to pieces easily.

We were frequently told that crocodiles carry leprosy germs in their teeth and several instances were quoted to us of people who had been bitten by crocodiles only to have gotten away, only to contract that dread disease some little time later. Anyway, I think that the bite of a crocodile would at least be septic owing to the putrid food they eat. On the other hand I have heard of blacks who are scarred as a result of their fights with crocodiles. Of course they may have leprosy, as we know that disease is rather prevalent among the natives.

Crocodiles are very timid and cowardly and, at the slightest sound, will glide into the water without making a noise or ripple. We therefore thought ourselves lucky when, on climbing the railway bridge near one end of the pool, we saw a crocodile near the bank further down. It was just beneath the surface with not much more than its eyes out of the water. Jack started off to get his rifle, but he had not gone many yards when I called out to him that the crocodile had disappeared.

Although we watched carefully a while longer, we did not see another sign of one. If we had seen that one before catching and cleaning the ducks we would not have acted so unconcernedly. When, a few miles further on, we camped for the night and cooked and ate those ducks, we thought they were well worth all the trouble they had cost us.

Side View of a Magnetic Ant-hill.

CHAPTER NINE

WE had thought when leaving Katherine to be in Darwin before this, but the road had been so rough and travelling so slow that we did not reach there until mid-day the following day. It had taken us four days to do a little over 200 miles, and we had been travelling from daybreak to dark. The last twenty miles of the road into Darwin presented no difficulties.

Darwin itself gave us a great surprise. We had expected to find a scattered collection of galvanised iron buildings. Instead, we found many fine stone buildings, beautiful homes, wide well-built streets, and the whole place a blaze of colour with the beautiful flowering shrubs and trees. Brilliant flame coloured poincianas, white and pink frangipanis, a tree with large yellow blooms of which I do not know the name, bougainvillea of various shades, and numerous other flowering trees and shrubs that I had never seen before.

Chinese form a large percentage of the population, and they own most of the shops, but they have their own quarters and are very unobtrusive and law-abiding.

There are also many blacks of various races here with a fair number of aborigines. A large aboriginal reserve is situated close to the town, and the blacks can be employed by the townsfolk for five shillings a week—two or three shillings being paid to the boy or lubra, and the balance to the Government on behalf of the employee.

Darwin is built on a bluff overlooking a fine harbour, and the approach from the sea should be very picturesque. Some beautiful beaches are to be found around Darwin, but one dare not bathe outside the swimming baths, as the sea is so infested with both sharks and crocodiles that between the two one wouldn't have much chance. It is fortunate for the shark that he has such speed at his command or he would very likely fall a prey to the crocodile, whose thick armour-like skin prevents the shark from attacking him.

Darwin is only a small place. I believe the white population is about one thousand. The town was founded in 1870 when the Northern Territory was under the control of South Australia. In 1911 the Territory was taken over by the Commonwealth. It is a vast state the area being 523,620 square miles. Much of it receives a good rainfall and is wonderfully fertile so that it should have a good future although, of course, its isolated position is a great handicap to it. In Darwin we had some of the most delicious mangoes we have ever tasted and we have sampled plenty in Queensland.

Among other places in Darwin we visited the Court House and were shown a collection of opium pipes that had been confiscated, each one having been an exhibit in a police court case. Opium smoking is against the law but, in spite of this, a fair amount of opium is smuggled in and smoked by the Chinese. They also have taught the aborigines to smoke and to them they sell their opium ash which is opium that has been once smoked but can be smoked again. Many of the aborigines are so addicted to the craze that they apparently spend every penny of their small earnings on opium or opium ash. They cannot afford to buy an opium pipe and their methods of making one are very ingenious.

With a red hot piece of wire they make a hole in the side of a bottle. The hole needed is only about as large as one a hat-pin would make. Into the neck of the bottle is fitted a piece of bamboo through which to draw the smoke. With a piece of wire they take out a small bead of opium which is a black semi-fluid substance like treacle but with a horrible smell. They twirl this around over a flame for a little while until it makes a ball then they poke the wire through the hole in the bottle so that the opium is left adhering all around the hole. This is then placed over a lamp and by sucking at the bamboo the opium is caused to smoulder and give off a smoke which very soon sends the smoker into a state of lethargy.

During our stay in Darwin we were taken by several friends to the Howard River for a picnic. We were particularly anxious to go as everyone told us this river was infested with crocodiles and Jack hoped to get a few skins. By the way, the people of the Territory never call them "crocodiles". They always refer to them as "alligators" or " 'gaters" but there are no real alligators found in Australia although there are several species of crocodiles.

We found the banks of the Howard River covered with dense jungle and working our way through this was no easy matter. Evidently the noise we made frightened away the crocodiles as we could not catch sight of any although we saw quite a number of their freshly made tracks in the mud.

It looked just the place for crocodiles. The heavy growth on the banks spread over the stream and dipped down into the water. Fallen trees were everywhere among the reeds and water-lilies in the stream. We had to balance ourselves on logs in order to get across out-jutting small channels filled with slimy oozes which, were you to fall in, would give up nothing of you but a few spasmodic gurgles.

The crocodile is very shy and a great coward and we were very surprised to hear how the niggers hunt it. If they find that a crocodile is in a certain pool a number of them will go in after it. They yell and beat the water making such a noise that the cowardly creature flees. When it is driven into shallow water the blacks surround it and spear it in a vital spot. Of course the flesh is eaten and it is considered a great luxury. We were told that it resembles pork.

There is a small species of crocodile that grows only about six feet long and is much relished by the blacks as an article of food. These are always called crocodiles to distinguish them from the larger ones which are always referred to as 'gaters. These small crocodiles are considered harmless, abound in certain fresh water pools and do not prevent either blacks or whites from going in for a bathe. However, we were never tempted to venture into the water where they were.

We enjoyed the week we spent in Darwin and made several good friends. We would have liked to have stayed longer but on every side we were hearing warnings about the approaching wet season. We were told that rain might come "any day" and many prophesied that we had not a possible chance of getting through before the floods.

The wet season in these parts is always preceded by a number of storms and after a week or two of these the real 'wet" comes when the rain comes down in torrents. During the wet all travelling is rendered very difficult and in most cases impossible through the whole of the country. Except in the town of Darwin there are no made roads and the ground becomes so saturated and soft that you can poke a stick down into it for several feet. In addition to the soft spongy nature of the ground another difficulty presents itself in the fact that every little watercourse becomes a surging torrent.

The people on the stations always take care to have large stocks of stores on hand so that they can wait quietly at home until the "wet" is over. The mailman goes on his route with his pack horses as long as he can but it gets too bad even for him and he has to join the army of the waiting.

One of the Many Rough Creek Crossings Between Katherine and Darwin

CHAPTER TEN

IT was with no feeling of pleasure that we started on the journey back to Katherine. Only once did we go astray and this time found ourselves in a timber-getters' camp but we had only gone a few miles out of our way.

I forgot to draw particular attention to the railway line that runs out from Darwin to Emungalen. It is not fenced in and, because of the possibility of buffaloes wandering on to the line, no travelling is done at night. The train only runs once a week and before dark it reaches the little station of Adelaide River (where there is a boarding house) on the journey one way and Pine Creek on the journey the other way. Some of the passengers go to the boarding house or hotel (if they are at Pine Creek) while the others camp wherever they can—in the train or on the ground nearby. In the morning the engine driver goes round and tells them all to hurry as the train is about to start. They don't get at all excited as they know that the train is not in the least like some of the disagreeable trains we have met and wouldn't think of starting without them. We were told that on occasions when fuel has been needed on the way the engine driver pulled up and all the men turned out and soon collected a heap of wood. Very strange this may sound to us but remember it is due to the efforts of pioneers such as these that a nation is built.

In Darwin we had met Mr. Hardy—a buffalo shooter—whose home is near Burrundie between Darwin and Katherine. He invited us to visit him on our return journey. We were doubtful if we would have the time but when one day we found ourselves near Burrundie just as the sun was setting we decided to avail ourselves of his hospitality and we were indeed glad that we were able to do so as Mr. and Mrs. Hardy and daughter made us so very welcome. We spent a most enjoyable evening listening to tales of the bush told as only a true bushman knows how to tell them. Mr. Hardy's accounts of the buffalo hunts were of especial interest.

Hubert "Fred" Hardy, buffalo hunter, Mt. Bundy station.

The buffaloes are to be found out in the swampy regions forty miles and more east of the railway line. The hunters steal up to the herd against the wind until the buffaloes become aware of the presence of the men and take to flight. Then the hunters charge on their horses and easily overtake the heavy lumbering buffaloes which are shot down one after another. The hunters aim for the spinal column and use a high-powered rifle with a very large bullet. They generally use a rifle with part of the barrel sawn off so that it can be used in one hand like a revolver. Of course it kicks like a mule but that isn't felt so much when the rifle is fired in the hand as it would be if it were held against the shoulder.

A wounded buffalo is a very dangerous enemy and Mr. Hardy told us of an experience he had with one. On that particular day he was riding a new horse unused to the work. I don't know exactly how it happened but the buffalo charged the horse breaking its leg and throwing Mr. Hardy to the ground. When the buffalo saw him it left the horse and rushed towards him. Luckily Mr. Hardy had the presence of mind to keep lying flat on the ground. Owing to the manner in which the buffalo's horns turn back it was unable to gore him whilst he kept in that position but it rolled him over with its nose blowing froth on him all the time. It is not very hard to imagine what his feelings must have been as he ran the risk of being trampled to death. Fortunately, the buffalo again caught sight of the horse which was struggling with its broken leg: so leaving its human victim which evidently wasn't proving very interesting, it hastened to put an end to the horse. Needless to say Mr. Hardy lost no time in making his escape and naturally he didn't feel like shooting any more buffaloes that day.

We passed such an interesting evening that, contrary to the custom of the bush, it was nearly midnight when we retired.

Early next morning we started off again on our race with the wet season although we would have enjoyed a longer stay with our kind host and hostess.

On the journey to Katherine our water tank developed a tiny leak. Every mile made it worse so we decided that we would have to stay in Katherine and mend it because ahead of us lay our longest waterless stages.

When Constable Clapp, whom we had met on the journey down, heard that we intended staying in Katherine for the night he insisted that we come and share his bachelor quarters.

We enjoyed our stay there very much. I took charge of the cooking and the constable expressed his delight at being relieved of this irksome task. It took some time to mend the leak so we were not ready to get away until about three o'clock the following afternoon. Just as we were ready to leave a storm came up so that our departure was delayed still further. We had been hurrying before but that storm which was the first of the forerunners of the wet season acted as a spur to us. It was five o'clock before the storm had subsided and we were able to leave Katherine.

We had afternoon tea (I should have said 'smoko'; before leaving so we decided not to stop for tea but to keep on driving until we were too tired to go any further then have something to eat before turning in for the night.

Once we were bogged in heavy sand (there had been very little rain here) which we would probably have been able to avoid in the day-time. It looked as though we would have to camp there until morning but with the aid of our spade we managed to get out.

We were becoming very hungry and sleepy but were keeping up as long as we possibly could. Suddenly we saw two white men standing in the middle of the track. It gave me quite a start as I thought no one was within many miles of us. The two men were travelling with pack horses to Tanami a new gold-field, and were camped for the night by the side of the track.

They invited us to have a cup of tea or cocoa and something to eat and we were so ravenously hungry that we just jumped at the invitation. I shall never forget that meal of damper, corned beef, pickles and cocoa taken seated on a pack-saddle about ten o'clock one night. I don't remember ever having appreciated a meal so much and I am sure I have never tasted a better damper. After our meal and a chat we felt so bucked up that we were able to drive another ten miles before turning in for the night. A big bush-fire had been through this part of the country so we were forced to make our camp among burnt stubble which was far from pleasant. The sky was still overcast so we slept in the car. We were glad too that we had done so as a sharp shower fell during the night.

Next morning dawned fine but we were not being lulled into any false sense of security and so wasted no time in getting under way.

About mid-day we arrived at Willeroo, one of Vestey's stations, where we had dinner but were, of course, unable to accept the manager's kind invitation to remain until the next day.

About ten miles past Willeroo I was driving when I felt a bump and heard something dragging behind. Pulling up immediately we discovered that a heavy box, which we had attached to the luggage carrier in Darwin and in which we had packed a number of things, had broken the luggage carrier with its weight and in falling had made two large holes in the water tank so that by the time we got to it all our water had leaked out on to the road. Our poor water tank seemed doomed. The next station was Victoria River Downs nearly a hundred miles away but Delamere an out-camp was only about twenty miles off so we made tor that.

We did not go any further than Delamere that night as we could not camp without water and were unable to repair our tank and luggage carrier at Delamere. We hoped, however to be able to fix them up at Victoria River Downs which, seeing that it has the reputation of being the largest station in the world, would be sure to have a blacksmith's shop where we could repair the damage.

The plain turkeys (properly called bustards) were very plentiful around here. After leaving Delamere next day we could easily have shot twenty or thirty but we only killed two to take into the next station with us as we often did. It is wonderful how close these turkeys will let you come in the car but several times in places where it was impossible to drive, we got out and tried to stalk them on foot but we might as well have saved ourselves the trouble as we couldn't get anywhere near them.

You do not have to be a good shot to hit a turkey from the car. If you miss with the first shot the bird either stares at the car as though wondering where the noise came from, or else begins to walk slowly away. We could usually have two or three shots at one (that was often necessary when I was shooting them with my little pea rifle) before it took to the wing.

CHAPTER ELEVEN

We arrived at Victoria River Downs early in the afternoon and we cannot say enough for the hospitality of the manager and his wife Mr. and Mrs. Martin. They had several children who looked the picture of health in spite of the contention that the north of Australia is not suitable for white people. After what we have seen on this trip, when we hear people make this statement it is to us like showing a red rag to a bull.

Victoria River Downs belongs to the Bovril Australian Estates, is over 13,000 square miles in area, and, we are told, has something like 150,000 head of cattle. It is fine country and better supplied with natural waters than the Barkly Tableland.

There is another Inland Mission Hospital here just about a quarter of a mile from the homestead.

The homestead is built on the bank of the Wickham a tributary of the Victoria River. In the dry season the river dwindles to a series of pools but the homestead is built on a permanent pool fifteen miles long and about a hundred yards wide. The water is splendid for drinking purposes and is pumped up and laid on all over the homestead and other buildings. Stores and supplies are brought twice a year by boat up the Victoria River as far as it is navigable to the Victoria River Depot and from there they are brought to the station by camel or donkey team. Sometimes it is not convenient to get the supplies by boat so then they have to be brought from the railhead at Emungalen.

When we arrived at the homestead stores were getting rather low and anxiety was being felt lest the supplies which were overdue should not arrive before the wet season. We were able to set their minds at rest on this point as, on the previous day, we had passed a donkey team with supplies for Victoria River.

Sometimes in the outback the stores run out before the fresh supplies arrive and people are compelled to live for some time practically on meat alone. Of course one gets terribly tired of an all meat diet but that is not the chief objection. It is liable to cause "Barcoo" which takes either of two forms. One form consists of severe attacks of vomiting and in the other, which I believe is the more common form, the skin begins to peel off in scales and sores break out. Many bushmen get this ailment from not eating sufficient vegetables, and to guard against this they nearly always have a fine vegetable garden on the stations. On the small places the cooks look after the garden, but on the large stations there is sometimes a gardener (often a chinaman) who does very little else.

Getting and laundry done was not nearly the trouble that I had expected it to be. Whenever we arrived at a station we would be invited to hand over anything that wanted washing to the lubras. These would think themselves well paid when we gave them each a couple of sticks of cheap tobacco, and the clothes would dry in a couple of hours even at night. The lubras around here had rather a peculiar way of using tobacco. They would chew it up and put the mass of chewed up tobacco in between the bottom lip and the gum where I suppose they get the flavour of it all the time. This causes the bottom lip to protrude a great distance and I wondered what I had struck when I saw the first one.

We sat around that evening listening to tales of the various people who had been seized by 'gaters or who had been killed by blacks in the district, one murder by the blacks having been committed only a few weeks previously. It was very interesting but perhaps not too good for one's nerves—mine at any rate. We had only been in bed about half an hour when I aroused the whole household by screaming and calling out at the top of my voice, "Jack! quick! quick! an alligator 's got me." It is not hard to guess what my dreams must have been.

It rained heavily for an hour or so that night and made us feel very anxious indeed although we were thankful to be in the homestead instead of being camped out fifty miles from nowhere.

There was a large camp of blacks just over the other side of the river and nearly all night long we could hear the sound of their corroberee.

All the corroboree songs we heard throughout the trip sounded practically the same although sung by so many different tribes. The weird low-toned penetrating drone of the didgeridoo their sole musical instrument, if it can be called such, could be heard above everything, The didgeridoo is a hollow wooden tube about two inches in diameter and from three to six feet in length. We understand that about five notes can be produced on it although we never heard more than two. Playing it is an art that requires practice as the player keeps the sound going continuously not even stopping every little while to take a breath. A bagpipe player has a reservoir of air but how the aboriginal keeps his drone going with out such assistance is a mystery. He must breathe in through his nose and out through his mouth at the same time if such a thing is possible.

After the storm the morning was fine but we knew it was useless to try to leave too early as we would only get bogged. A few hours of bright sunshine would make a great difference to the ground so about midday. Jack having repaired our luggage carrier and water tank, we set off. How we would have loved to have stayed for a few days at Victoria River Downs but delay would have been foolish. Every storm seemed to be getting worse and we had many big rivers ahead of us. Especially had we been warned about the Fitzroy which, if it were to become flooded, would be uncrossable for from four to five months and we would be held up all that time. This was not a pleasant prospect so it is no wonder that we hurried.

We left well laden with corned beef, bread, cake and produce of the garden. The hospitable folk on the stations always treated us like this giving us at least enough fresh meat and bread to see us to the next station. Even where the next station was within easy reach they would insist on our taking something with us in case we were held up in some way.

There was a rough track between Victoria River and Wave Hill, the next station, about a hundred miles away. An out-camp of Victoria River Downs was forty miles from the homestead but we hoped to get a good deal past there that day. Travelling was very heavy as the ground was still rather mushy and we had to dodge many bog-holes but, by keeping on the high ground, we managed to make good progress.

About thirty-five miles from Victoria River Downs we found our path blocked by a creek—only a little one a few yards wide, but it was a black soil creek and badly silted. We walked up and down the bank but could find no way of getting across. This creek, except in the wet season, presents no difficulty as it is nearly always dry but on this particular day it was running as a result of the storm the previous night.

I put a stick in the ground and found that the water was falling rapidly so I suggested camping on the bank and crossing the creek in the morning. Had we done as I suggested we would never have got through before the "big wet". Jack, however, knew more of the bush than I did and said, "There is only one side to camp on and that is the other side". He picked the narrowest and shallowest part and drove the car in until she settled down with her running boards and back axle in the water and mud. We had chains on the wheels but they were useless because of the depth of the silt. We had brought a wire rope and small winch with us for such situations as this so, by attaching the rope to a tree and with a good deal of hard work, we finally got the car on to firm ground again.

Three miles further on we came to "Pigeon Hole," the out-station. We had wasted so much time at the creek that it was almost dark when we arrived there so, as there was a possibility of striking more boggy places, we did not go any further that night.

Well Bogged Near Pigeon Hole.

About 10 o'clock that evening it started to rain and rained steadily until day-break. By that time our spirits were just about down to zero. Leaving that day was out of the question as we were told that several bad creeks would block our way. Although we were feeling pretty blue at being held up like this we were delighted at having crossed that creek instead of being camped on the other side of it.

A cook was in charge at Pigeon Hole which is a sort of depot for the stockmen and station hands when they are in that part of the run. The cook told us that he had practically no food supplies left. He had a small bag of flour, three or four pounds of sugar, and about half a pound of tea in the place. He did not have an ounce of such things as rice, sago, or tapioca. We were carrying supplies that would last the two of us for about a month but, as there were several others there besides ourselves, it would not help matters much although, of course, we would pool our resources in the event of our being held up for any length of time.

All day long we watched those heavy clouds and how delighted we were that no more rain fell. The goats' milk at Pigeon Hole was as bitter as if it had had quinine added to it. They told us that this was caused by the goats' eating a shrub called Leichhardt.

Donkey team with goods for Victoria River Downs.

CHAPTER TWELVE

The following morning dawned fine, and no rain having fallen during the night, we were able to leave Pigeon Hole. We took with us Mr. McGugan, the manager of Wave Hill station, whom we had found at Pigeon Hole and who was pleased of the lift home.

The black soil was exceedingly heavy from the rain and travelling was very slow for the first twenty miles. After that we found that not so much rain had fallen although for many miles we were dodging slushy holes that would have bogged us badly if we had got into them. In one of these we found a poor cow bogged. Jack and Mr. McGugan managed to pull her out but the first thing she did was to charge them. They tell me that bogged cattle always show their gratitude in this way. She was too weak to do any damage and after a few steps she fell down again.

We were warned that we might get bogged at Longreach Crossing but we came through without the least trouble as this was a sandy place and had been much improved by the rain. Here we camped and boiled the billy for dinner.

About eight miles before getting into Wave Hill we ran into a pretty heavy storm and were rather worried as we were on black soil. Although we were making as much speed as possible, still, when we saw four turkeys, Jack couldn't resist taking a shot at them. He quickly secured two and we arrived at Wave Hill before the really heavy part of the storm came.

It continued to rain for a couple of hours so we were forced to remain at the station all night. Although we were terribly worried because it looked as though the wet season was overtaking us, we could not fail to enjoy our stay there especially with such a kind host as Mr. McGugan.

We were surprised to find a wireless transmitting station at Wave

Hill with a P.M.G. man in charge so we were able to send a radiogram home. Wave Hill is another of Vesteys' stations, and is, I believe, somewhere about 8000 square miles in area. Vestey Bros, have a very large number of stations in the Northern Territory and Western Australia. In Darwin we visited their fine meat works which are now idle and in which the sum of £1,000,000 has been invested.

There are a large number of blacks around Wave Hill. A tribe of about 400 live around the station and there is a big camp of them just over the creek from the homestead. Some of them are employed by the station and these are fed but the others live on whatever they can kill.

The present homestead of Wave Hill has been recently built, as the old homestead, which was some five miles away from the present site, was washed away by an extra big flood a year or two ago. Homesteads are usually built close to permanent water and we heard of several cases where the flood rises up to or into the house nearly every year.

Mr. McGugan told us a very amusing story about the Wave Hill flood which washed away the homestead. The tribe there has its rain-maker, without whom no tribe would be complete. There had been no rain for a long time, so Mr. McGugan thought he would have a joke with the rain-maker and said. "Jacky, waterhole all dry up—you go up river, makem rain, fillem up waterholes". Jacky went off and, the wet season being due, rain did come, so much in fact that the ensuing flood swept away the homestead and nearly all the out-buildings. The white people there spent some very anxious hours on top of the buggy shed which was the highest point.

After the flood Jacky was heard to say. Boss him bin plurry fool sendem me UP river makem rain. S'posin' him bin sendem me DOWN river no bin makeit flood".

Among the men on top of the buggy shed was Mr. Moray the superintendent of Vesteys' stations. Slung across his shoulder all the time he had his camera loaded with a spool of films, but so anxious were they all and so little hope did they entertain of living through that flood that he did not think to take a single snap and afterwards regretted the wonderful opportunities he missed. We can sympathize with you Mr.

Moray! What a number of wonderful photographs we missed in the same manner.

After tea the sound of the corroboree song was wafted across from the camp about half a mile away. Jack and I had always been anxious to see a corroboree, so taking a hurricane lamp with us, we went over to the scene of the festivities.

We first came to a number of gunyahs. A lubra came out of one of these (she was one of the house gins) and we asked her if we could see the corroboree or "playabout" as the half-civilized ones call it. While around the house the blacks are compelled to wear clothes but it was an oppressive evening so here, in the camp, she had discarded everything except a little bit of a skirt. We gave her a stick of tobacco and a red handkerchief and she conducted us over to the corroboree.

She was carrying a little piccaninny a month or two old. It was lying asleep in a "coolimon" which is a boat-shaped wooden vessel made from portion of a tree trunk. She carried it on one hip with a cord slung around her neck to take part of the weight. Besides doing service as a cradle coolimons are used for almost anything that a dish might be used for. Water or food is carried in them and sometimes the gins turn them into mixing bowls in which to mix rough cakes of ground up seeds or nardoo. By other tribes we have heard a "coolimon" referred to as a "pitchi" or a "tarcoola".

The piccaninny this lubra carried was a dear little thing but terribly dirty. This impression was given chiefly by the thick cake of dirt on its head. The front part of its scalp was covered with what looked like a mass of grease and dirt about a quarter of an inch thick. Jack suggested that this was probably put on purposely to protect that tender portion of the baby's skull and it certainly seems very likely.

The corroboree was of a very primitive nature. The gins were all lined up on one side and they formed a sort of an accompaniment rather than an actual part of the corroboree. Each gin held in her hands a piece of string, (the blacks can make rough twine from fibres) vine or supple branch. She grasped this with both hands, the object of it evidently being to keep the hands about the width of the shoulders apart while she swung her arms from side to side. While doing this arm movement each gin shuffled her feet in a manner greatly resembling the Charleston step. When one gin would tire she would step out and another from a group behind would quickly get into the line and take her place.

The music for this performance was supplied by the orchestra seated in a ring on the ground. There was the didgeridoo, which I explained before, and several boys with bones or sticks which they beat together, all keeping the same monotonous time.

The actual dancers were the men (chiefly the younger ones) who pranced about doing all the time the same high leg action and now and then singing in their own language snatches of their corroboree song.

There was a great deal of hissing too and stamping of feet. The dance seemed to consist of a number of figures. Every few minutes the dancers would stop and laugh and all talk at once—they were evidently enjoying themselves immensely. Sometimes they would dance with all the weapons they could lay their hands on and the way they brandished them and the threatening attitudes they assumed made us almost wish we were at home in bed. Often at the end of a little dance they would finish up in a close group flinging their arms into the air and letting out piercing shrieks. It was wonderful how quickly they could change from savage looking warriors to little more than laughing children.

Some had their bodies and faces painted. Others were decorated with feathers, while others again had small bunches of leaves tied on to their legs and wrists.

Jack sat down in the orchestra next to a savage looking chap with a painted face and white cockatoo feathers in his hair. I stood up behind—ready to run. Every time they would finish a dance we would loudlv proclaim that it was "good-fellow good-fellow" (we felt it best to keep on the good side of them). They were immensely pleased at our praise and seemed to take our presence as a great compliment.

Of course it was only an ordinary corroboree that we witnessed. They often have sacred corroborees at which none of the gins or uninitiated boys are allowed to be present.

Corroborees are held for many reasons. The ordinary corroborees or "playabouts" are solely a recreation; sacred corroborees are for the purpose of appeasing or frightening debil-debils; other corroborees are supposed to bring emus, kangaroos, or game about in large numbers. In addition to these there are the dances of the different totems, as each black is supposed to have an animal's spirit within him and that places him in a certain totem or class.

The boys of the tribe live with the gins until they are about twelve years of age. Then they are taken charge of by the men, and when about fourteen they are put through a period of trial and initiation into all the sacred rites of the tribe. This ceremony the partly civilized ones call "makeit young man" and after that the boy takes his place as a full-grown man, warrior and hunter. Of course, as the tribes become more and more civilized these customs gradually fall into disuse.

The old homestead of Wave Hill was situated at the foot of a hill which had peculiar horizontal outcroppings of strata at almost regular intervals. From some distance away this gives the impression of waves hence the name of the station. We left Wave Hill after "smoko" the next morning, once more regretful that circumstances compelled us to hurry. Mr. McGugan saw that we were well supplied with fresh provisions as the next station was about 140 miles away. Before leaving Wave Hill we collected three drums of petrol that had been waiting there for us for several months.

There is a police station at Wave Hill near the site of the old homestead. The police of the Northern Territory are an exceptionally fine body of men. They are held in great fear and respect by the natives owing to their success in capturing the perpetrators of the various crimes that have been committed, and, because of the efficiency of the police, even the myall (wild) niggers realize what will happen to them if they harm the white man or touch his belongings.

The white population of the Territory is about 3000 while the black population is set down at somewhat over 20,000 although, owing to the number of uncivilized wandering tribes, there is no way of arriving at anything like a correct estimate. Seeing that the whites are so outnumbered it is just as well for their peace that the blacks regard the police with such awe.

CHAPTER THIRTEEN

AFTER leaving Wave Hill we had dinner at a large water-hole at a place called Bow Hills. We walked along the bank to see if we could find any ducks but we could not see any. Just as we were about to turn away we discovered a fine healthy-looking young cow bogged at the edge of the hole right at the bottom of a very steep bank. On the top of the bank was a tiny calf only a day or two old. Although we could ill afford to waste any time we simply could not go away and leave that poor cow to die by inches and the little calf also to perish.

But how to get her out was a problem. She was a large heavy cow and the bank was from ten to twelve feet high and so nearly perpendicular that we found great difficulty in climbing down it. Jack fastened the wire rope around her horns with the intention of pulling her out with the car. I was rather inclined to give it up as a bad job as I thought it was too much to expect the car, which was already carrying a load of about 18 cwt., to pull that cow up the sheer bank as well. But I was wrong. First we pulled her free from the mud, then a long steady pull brought her right to the top of the bank.

The outer shell of one of her horns was broken in the process, but we thought that was a small matter compared with a lingering death. By lifting her by the tail Jack brought her to her feet and, strange to relate, she didn't charge him. We went back to our dinner and a few minutes later saw the cow walking off with her calf. She evidently had not been in the bog very long or she would have lost the use of her legs.

That night we camped 65 miles from Wave Hill. We were on the look-out for the Gee Bee Rockhole of which we had been told but we could not find it. Our tank full of water, however, was more than sufficient for our needs.

Practically no rain had fallen here which fact cheered us up quite a lot. There was a great deal of thunder and lightning that night but not a spot of rain. From here on to Inverway (the next station) the patches of desert, which we found interspersed with the black soil plains, afforded some of the finest travelling surfaces over which I have ever driven. This desert country was composed of a dark red (almost black) sandy soil and was as firm and smooth as a newly-built bitumen road. We were surprised to hear that when this soil is properly wet it is worse than black soil. It doesn't stick, but it has no bottom to it, so that it is impossible even for horses to travel over it when wet, to say nothing of the car.

We were following a distinct track, but it was painfully crooked. It had been made originally by the camel trains which always took the line of least resistance and dodged in and out among the bushes. The result certainly was the most crooked track I have ever seen.

About mid-day we arrived at Inverway, which is owned by the three Farquharson Brothers. Only one of them was at home, but he made us very welcome and gave us an enjoyable dinner. Mr. Farquharson was the only white man we met in 300 miles of travelling. What a lonely life they lead, with their nearest neighbour 140 miles away.

After dinner we set out on one of the longest stages of our trip. The next place would be Flora Valley, nearly two hundred miles away, and for the greater part of this journey water was unprocurable. These long stages are nothing to a motor car as long as the car keeps going, but in the event of a breakdown, entailing a walk of fifty miles or more without water, we would have a bad time, for the weather was excessively hot and we had not trained ourselves to go on a short allowance of water. We just had to put our trust in the little car, and she proved well worthy of it. Not once on the whole trip did anything go wrong with the mechanism.

About 32 miles from Inverway we came to a large waterhole in a creek called Wallamunga. If I attempt to describe the number of ducks we saw there you will most surely disbelieve me. There were more wild ducks than I thought existed in the whole of Australia, which could perhaps be accounted for by the fact that it was the end of the dry season, and that waterhole probably contained the only water within many, many miles.

The hole must have been about a mile and a half long. Some thousands of ducks were in the water, but they were nothing compared with the number on the banks, each bank was lined with ducks about ten or fifteen deep, sitting close together along the whole length of the waterhole. There were only a few trees near the waterhole, so that we could not creep up unobserved and get a shot with the little rifle, for as soon as the ducks saw us they rose shrieking in immense clouds. Those on the far bank were not much perturbed, but they were too far away for a shot with the pea rifle.

Jack said that he would climb up a tree on the bank and hide among the branches, while I went further up the stream and scared the ducks there down towards him, so that he could get a shot at them. Howbeit, our scheme didn't work, such is the perversity of nature, for that, although the ducks had risen in fear at the sight of us creeping up to the hole, now they simply refused to fly when I walked openly up to them. They would just rise and fly a few yards further away. After that I stamped, yelled, and threw stones at them, but couldn't make them move more than a few feet at a time.

I kept walking down the stream at the edge of the water, chasing the ducks and looking for Jack, while he having got tired of sitting in the tree, had started up-stream after me. I must have walked about a mile without seeing him, and he had gone up some distance in the opposite direction looking for me, but he had walked along the top of the bank and so missed me at the water's edge.

I then tried to go back to the car, but it had disappeared, Jack having by then taken it to go and look for me. The sun was just dipping behind the horizon and I was feeling very frightened at the prospect of being lost all night. There was a large open plain near the creek, so I walked out on to that and Jack saw me. I could have cried with relief when I saw the car coming in my direction. I had been worried, but Jack was nearly frantic. He knew that I had no bush experience and thought that I had followed another arm of the creek and got lost, and getting lost there, where there are not even fences to guide one. would mean almost certain death.

We drove on a few miles and camped just inside Western Australia. It was too dark to see the cairn of stones which marks the border, but we must have been well past it, judging by the distance we had come.

We had to use our water very sparingly that night as we would get no more for about a hundred miles and we did not know what kind of country was ahead of us.

We slept on the ground, but were very much annoyed by ants —only small black ones, but they crawled over us and bit us. Previously we had never been worried by ants at night, although they had often been bad in the day-time, but these Western Australian ants must have worked in shifts as they kept going all night long. We found this the case right through Western Australia. Jack explained that ants are usually bad in sandy country, and that seems to account for it, as sandy country certainly is the type most prevalent in Western Australia.

The road surface was fair all next day, and we made good progress. That afternoon we saw some turkeys strutting about with their tails spread out like peacocks', their neck feathers all fuzzed up, and the feathers on their breasts drooped almost to the ground. We thought at first that it was some special variety of turkey, but we shot a couple and found they were just ordinary plain turkeys or bustards. Furthermore, we noticed that whenever a turkey was strutting like this, a smaller bird, evidently the turkey hen, was somewhere in the vicinity, so we came to the conclusion that this was their manner of courting.

When we got to within three or four miles of Flora Valley, we found that heavy rain had just fallen there. Several times we had to go through boggy-looking places, but the ground had not had time to get properly soaked, so we got through without any trouble and arrived just about sundown at Flora Valley which was a pretty place at the foot of a range of mountains. Mr. and Mrs. Chidley (the manager and his wife) extended to us the hearty welcome of the bush.

They had a wonderful dog; just an ordinary blue cattle dog, but if it were in America I am sure it would be figuring in some of the movie films. This dog, Bluey, seemed to everything that was said to him and would go and bring whatever article he was told to get and would also put things away wherever he was told to put them. Whenever he was hungry he would go and get a little billy-can that was always kept for him, and would sit patiently holding it in his mouth until some food was put into it. Then Bluey would go outside, tip the food out, and eat it. If he wanted more all he had to do was to bring his billy-can back again, with the result that he was a very fat dog.

The dinner-bell was fitted with a leather strap instead of a handle, for ringing the bell was Bluey's job. When he was told to ring it he would take the strap in his mouth, walk round and ring the bell in front of everyone. Although we were strangers, he came round and, standing in front of each of us in turn, rang the bell vigorously.

It rained thirty points that night. We were upset at finding that the storms were catching up to us, for we thought we had left them behind. We were not, however, held up by the two storms that had fallen here as the track to Hall's Creek, they told us, was very stony and very hilly. Even to call it "very hilly" is to express it mildly, as it proved to be thirty miles of the most hilly country I have ever seen.

In that part of the world Hall's Creek is looked upon as a town —I don't know what city dwellers would call it. We found there a store, hotel, post office, police station, and an Inland Mission Hospital—nothing else. Still, those few places are a boon in the outback and we were glad to find a store where we could get supplies and also a post office where we received and sent telegrams.

There are still a few old prospectors looking for gold around here, and many people are confident that the Kimberleys will boom again as gold is still to be found there. We were told that the chief reason of the failure of the Kimberley goldfield was the high cost of transport as goods had to be brought out by camel or donkey team from Derby (four hundred miles away), and the travelling was some of the most difficult that we experienced on the whole trip. It cost somewhere about £100 a ton for cartage alone to land provisions in Hall's Creek. If a road were built with proper crossings over the sandy rivers, so that the carting could be done by motor truck, the cost of cartage would be only about £ 20 a ton.

A shop front in Winton, celebrating the actor Rudolph Valentino, who died on August 23 1926.

CHAPTER FOURTEEN

THAT afternoon we went only as far as Moola Bulla. We had intended going further, but Mr. and Mrs. Woodland proved so very kind and hospitable. and the homestead looked so comfortable, that we could not resist the temptation to remain there overnight. It was lucky for us that we did, for it rained heavily during the night and we would have had a most unpleasant camp in the open.

Moola Bulla is a Government cattle station, the object of it being to breed cattle from which to supply the natives with meat, and also to provide employment for the natives. The blacks know they can get meat here, and it has done much towards preventing cattle- killing by the natives. The name "Moola Bulla' means "plenty beef' and sometimes they are feeding as many as three hundred aborigines there. The station is so complete that it is almost a township. There is even a sawmill and tannery in addition to what is usually found on a large station.

Contrary to the usual custom, there is a woman cook at Moola Bulla, and Jack and I agree that she makes the finest bread we have ever tasted. I won't mention the name of the place where we got the worst bread, but I will tell you about it. Passing through a small town, we managed to buy a loaf of bread. When we camped that night Jack took the stale loaf of bread (about four days old) out of the tucker-box and threw it away among the bushes. When we tasted the new bread it was so coarse and sour that we hastily threw it away and retrieved our stale loaf, which tasted sweet by comparison.

Owing to the rain during the night, we thought it would be unwise to leave Moola Bulla until the ground had a chance to dry a little. We spent the morning watching a black boy named "Wallaby" riding some buckjumpers, and in looking over the blacks' camp, where we collected some fine souvenirs.

We were always very much amused at some of the funny names the blacks have. They, of course, have their own aboriginal names, but these are so difficult to pronounce that the whites give them new names when they come to work on the stations. Many have ordinary Christian names, but some of them are really funny being more like the names for dogs or horses than anything else. Some of the blacks we met were called: Whalebone, Kiwi, Bootlace, Snowball, Ruler, Nugget, Charcoal, Sunbeam. Sparrow, Bandy, Cockeye, Emu-foot, Larrikin and Miss Australia. The blacks in most cases are blissfully ignorant of the meanings of their English names.

The natives were quite ready to barter their weapons and implements for pipes, sticks of tobacco, or red handkerchiefs. When we picked up some string made of human hair, the gin who owned it thought fiat we intended taking it, and came running up in a great state. She offered us anything else, but nothing could induce her to part with that. hair. It was probably being woven up as a gift for a son-in-law. She was a very young gin, but even if her piccaninny were only a few weeks old, that piccaninny (if a female) would probably be promised in marriage and the future son-in-law would enter on his rights as son-in-law immediately, one of which privileges is certain claims to his mother-in-law's hair. As far as we could make out, a son-in-law, even if he is only a prospective one, seems to have more claim on a woman's hair than her own husband.

Besides the power that hair has of keeping away "debil-debils," they believe it can cure headaches and pains, and is, in fact, just teeming with magic. Doubltess, if we had a belt that would keep us well and strong and free from all harm, we wouldn't be too ready to part with It either.

We often wondered how the blacks fastened their spear-heads on to the. spears. In the camp at Moola Bulla we saw some spinifex wax which is used for that purpose. The lump we saw was a very hard, dirty brown substance, almost like a piece of brick to look at. We were told that it is made of the gums and oozes from a variety of plants and trees, and to be prepared, has to be masticated for some time. This task, of course, falls to the lubras. When heated, the wax becomes soft and it hardens again when cold.

Among other things, we procured a nulla-nulla—a smooth (looking almost as if it were polished) round stick about three feet long and one and a half inches in diameter. It is made of very heavy wood and looks a formidable weapon. We were surprised to learn that a black thinks nothing of giving his wife a whack over the head with one. Such a blow would probably kill a white woman, or, at any rate, render her unconscious, but the blacks have skulls like iron. Sometimes, when one is contemplating marriage with a lubra, he will put her to a test by giving her a heavy blow with a nulla-nulla. If she falls beneath the stroke she is not worthy to be his wife. How fortunate for us white women that our men do not adopt similar methods of wooing!

We left Moola Bulla after, an early lunch and, for a couple of hours, struck no difficulties. Then we ran into a storm. We did not get much rain, but we could see that heavy rain was falling some distance away on our right. The storm was just over when we came to a little creek that blocked our path. It was only ten yards wide, but it was running a banker, obviously from the storm that had just fallen. Jack waded in, but the water was up to his waist, so, as this was too deep for a motor car, there was nothing else to do but wait for the flood to subside. We put a peg in the bank and were relieved to find that the water was already falling. In about an hour's time the stream had gone down sufficiently for us to attempt to cross.

Jack had to take it very steadily for the bank was steep, the water still fairly deep, and the bed of the creek was composed of loose, soft sand which was being swirled about by the fast running water. We got a little past the middle of the stream, but there we stuck with the water coming right over the running boards.

Quickly we both set to work to take off the heavy items of the load and carry them to the bank in order to lighten the car and give her a chance of pulling herself out. The wheels were buried deep into the sand, but by scraping this away from the front of each wheel we were able to drive her forward a few inches. Then the sand would set firmly around the wheels again, and we would have to repeat the same performance. In this way, by alternately driving and digging, we got her out, a few inches at a time.

Whenever we were in difficult situations Jack always drove while I got out and pushed. This wasn't because, he believed in making the woman do the work, but he was so much better at driving than I, that he was able to get much more out of the car.

We loaded up as quickly as we could, for we were trying to reach the Margaret Station, seventy miles from Moola Bulla, before night.

We had gone only three miles when we found that the track we were following crossed again over the creek that had given us so much trouble. This creek had meandered a great deal between the first and second crossing and had also received a tributary, so that we found the second crossing in about the same state as we had found the first. This meant that we had to wait again, so we took advantage of the delay to have our tea. By the time we had finished, the water had subsided to a few inches in depth, and, although the stream here was twice as wide as at the first crossing, we went across without the least difficulty owing to the firmer nature of the sand and the fact that it was not being swirled about by a strong current.

We crossed over a couple of large river beds that evening, but we had no further trouble. One was a large, dry, sandy bed, the appearance of which was very alarming, but our little car never baulked once In the other—the Laura River—the water was just beginning to run.

We arrived at the Margaret Station about eight o'clock, and Mr. J. Egan (the manager) made us welcome at once. There were only two white men here—the manager and the cook. They told us that the Margaret River was in flood and was rising and, very likely, we would not be able to cross on the morrow. This was made a certainty by heavy rain falling for several hours that night.

Unless you have tried it, you have no conception of how despondent it makes one feel to hear heavy rain falling when one is camped on the bank of a large river that is rapidly rising. Every day we could see that a number of storms fell somewhere round about, even though they might not fall where we happened to be. The monsoonal rain was likely to start any moment or a rapid sequence of storms hold us prisoners until it arrived.

We did not relish this possibility as it would mean our being held up four or five months as, owing to the soft ground and flooded rivers, it is impossible to travel—-especially by motor car—until some time after the rain ceases. If we were to be held up we would be fortunate indeed if we were on a station, but we could easily be made prisoners between two rivers, when we would just have to pick the highest ground we could find and have a very unpleasant camp for a few months, if we were lucky enough not to get washed away. We were carrying a fairly large stock of provisions, but in the event of our having to camp we would be dependent chiefly on our guns. No one, most likely, would know of our plight, except perhaps a few walkabout blacks.

The people ahead would not know of our existence, and those we had left would not know that we had been unable to get through. If we had been held up like this, what anxiety we would have caused our people back home, for we would have been unable to get word to them for so long. Of course, we thought of all these unpleasant things while it was raining during the night, so that it was a pretty gloomy pair who turned up for breakfast next morning. However, it cheered us up wonderfully to think that, for the present, anyway, we were under shelter, and our kind host didn't seem at all concerned at the prospect of having us on his hands for several months.

The Margaret River was only a few hundred yards away from the house, but the only place where it was possible to cross was seven miles from the homestead.

About nine o'clock the morning after our arrival a black brought us word that the river was falling. This information, added to the fact that the sky was much clearer, made our spirits rise considerably.

When we arrived at the Margaret Station we had noticed a number of aboriginals huddled in the cart-shed. Mr. Egan told us that the blacks were most uncanny weather prophets, and explained that for the greater part of the year they camped down on the sand near to or in the river bed. The previous night they had deserted their camp and come up on the high ground near the house, saying that the river was going to rise that night. How they knew this he could not tell, but, sure enough, their forecast proved correct, for when he woke the next morning the river was in flood.

From nine o'clock the river still continued to fall, so, after an early lunch, Mr. Egan and Jack went down in the car to see the condition of the river at the place where we would have to cross. They took several blacks with them and they did not get back until dusk, when they arrived with themselves and the car simply covered with mud. It had only rained one and a half inches at the homestead, but Mr. Egan said that at least four inches must have fallen a couple of miles away.

They had driven across flats which, for the time being, were converted into swamps and they had been bogged many times. One little creek—a tributary of the Margaret—held them up for a long time, as it was just full of sandy silt. The blacks had worked splendidly and were delighted when they were rewarded with a few sticks of tobacco.

Jack had managed to drive right down to the river, where they found about four feet of water, but Mr. Egan thought that, at the rate it was falling, it would be shallow enough for us to get across the next day. He told us that we wouldn't have the faintest hope of getting across the Margaret without help, so he kindly picked out five strong black boys and sent them down to the river early on the following morning, there to await our arrival so as to give us assistance.

Moola-Bullo, the Girl's Quarters

CHAPTER FIFTEEN

WE got away as early as possible as we knew that we had a big day's work ahead of us. We were very amused at a black boy who opened the gate for us as we were leaving the horse-paddock. He had absolutely not a stitch of clothing on, but had a long heavy string of rosary beads around his neck. I have no idea where he got them, but he certainly thought he was handsomelyfittedout.

At the three mile creek (the one which had given Jack and Mr. Egan so much trouble the previous day) we found three of the boys waiting for us. Two of them had come down with the car the previous day and had helped a great deal in picking branches to put under the wheels to make a path out of the bog. Here, at the creek, we found that the boys had profited by their experience of the previous day, as they had pulled a number of branches and leaves and had made a path right across the creek, so that we were able to cross without the least trouble.

The Margaret River here was about two hundred yards wide. A channel of water about fifty yards wide. was running near the far bank, and we found that this water was just shallow enough to allow us to cross. We first got some of the boys to cut down part of the bank so as to allow the car to be driven into the river at a fair speed. While they were doing this we took all the heavy articles off the car and gave them to the other boys to carry across. When all was ready, Jack stationed the boys at the part where the sand was heaviest and where he thought the car would be likely to slow down, and gave them instructions to push when the car got up to them.

Jack then rushed the car into the bed of the river at as high a speed as the roughness of the bank would permit. The loose heavy sand slowed the car down and, although she struggled on bravely, she was eventually brought to a standstill. Anyhow, we had crossed fifty or sixty yards of the river without the assistance of the boys, which was much more than we had hoped to do.

Then Jack and the boys set to work scraping away the sand and picking branches to put under the wheels to provide a firm grip for them and so enable the car to start off once again. We were only held up once more before reaching the channel of water, for the dry sand was not nearly as bad as the wet sand which was so loose and soft that it was almost like quicksand. The five boys pushed with all their might and. even then, we had several times to stop and dig the wheels out before reaching the far bank which proved the toughest problem of all. It was high and steep and consisted of a mixture of sand and mud, so that the wheels could hardly get a grip and the engine was almost useless.

Jack drove and the five boys all pushed at once; and. as the car went forward a little, I shoved a log under the back wheels to prevent us from losing the few inches so hardly won, and bit by bit we struggled up that bank.

We had crossed the river successfully, but Mr. Egan had told us that we would have to cross it again about three miles further on, as there was a bend in the stream, and he also informed us that the second crossing of the Margaret was far worse than the first. The boys had worked splendidly, so we gave them each a present of a clay pipe, a couple of sticks of tobacco, and a box of matches. We had wrapped the clay pipes in tissue paper to keep them from breaking, and we gave them to the boys still wrapped up. We noticed afterwards that, whenever they put the pipes back into their pockets, they would first of all carefully wrap them in the tissue paper. How simple their wants and what a little it took to please them! Those pipes that they prized so much had cost us a mere 2p each.

We told the boys to walk on to the second crossing while we loaded up the car. Having done this we drove on and overtook them just as they were nearing the second crossing. This crossing proved even worse than we had expected to find it, as it was much wider and had two channels of water instead of one. The boys worked wonderfully getting the car across. The sand was more troublesome than in the first crossing, but we struggled across the first channel, and with a deal of work got the car over the stretch of sand dividing the two channels. As we approached the second channel the wheels sank further and further into the soft sand, until, by the time we reached the edge of the water, they were so firmly embedded that the greatest efforts of the engine and the boys could not move the car. There was nothing to do now but take the heavy items of the load off, dig the sand away, and put branches under the wheels.

While the boys were working with the car, I made a fire, and, by the time they had got the car across, I had a couple of billycans of tea ready. As the blacks had a ten-mile walk back to the station, we could not let them go back without a billy of tea and something to eat. We had brought a good supply of bread from the station, so I opened a large tin of meat and gave us some sandwiches which they voted "goodfella."

The boys had been working for us from daylight until mid-day. and altogether the things we had given them cost us about four shillings — remarkably cheap labour, especially considering the strenuous nature of the work. The boys, however, thought that they had been treated very generously, and were delighted with the presents they had received.

Once across the Margaret we made all the speed we could, our object being the Fitzroy River, well over a hundred miles away. The Margaret, we knew, was a tributary of the Fitzroy, and, as it had been flooded, we were in great fear that we would find the Fitzroy in the same condition. Before we reached it, however, there were many more rivers and creeks to be crossed!

All the rest of that day we were having to reconnoitre to find our way around swamps, and some of the creeks proved very troublesome. One little creek I shall never forget. It was only about fifteen yards wide, but had just enough water running in it to make the sand like quicksand, even worse than the channels of the Margaret. For about an hour Jack swung an axe chopping down all the bushes nearby, while I carried them and made two thick tracks for our wheels. We did not want to waste time by unloading the car, so our only chance was to take the creek at a high speed. This, however, was a risky procedure, owing to the fact that there was a drop of a foot or eighteen inches into the creek. Jack went back a bit to get a run at it, and jumped the Whippet into that creek at thirty miles an hour. The jar was terrific and several items of the load flew out of the car, whilst Jack received a blow on the back of the head with the camera tripod, which nearly put him out of the race. I stood on the bank anxiously watching and expected to see some part of the car break down under such harsh treatment, but when we examined it we found that not a single thing was broken—not even a spring leaf. It is not hard to imagine how concerned we were about the car, seeing the serious position we were in.

A couple of other creeks which looked really treacherous did not hinder us at all. One fair-sized sandy creek gave us a good deal of trouble, as several teams had just crossed over it. Following a track made by a team is infinitely worse than having no track at all. The waggon tracks are a few inches wider than a motor track, so, if you drive with a wheel of your car in one of the team tracks, you have your other wheel in the loose sand that has been heaped up by the other wheel of the waggon. The donkeys' feet, too, dig up the loose sand, making it a great deal worse. A little further on we came to a couple of donkey teams and a camel team which were just about to pull up for the night. These teams were hauling an oil prospecting plant, and were turning south not far from where we met them, so they would not have to cross the Fitzroy. Nearly all the carting in the remote places is done by donkey or camel team, and we met several of each at different times. The donkeys are hardy little animals, very quiet and sensible. They soon learn to know their exact places, even in a team of forty or fifty, and, when rounded up in the morning, will go and stand in their correct positions waiting for the collars to be put on. The harness of each donkey is left on the ground just where it is taken off. Travelling by donkey team is very slow, as, I believe, they average somewhere about twelve miles a day; camels would do a little more, perhaps about fifteen. The camel team we saw here consisted of about eighteen camels yoked like horses.

The harness consisted of ordinary horse harness with the collar and harness upside down Why this was done I do not know, but I came to the conclusion that camels in harness looked about the most awkward things I had ever seen. They were driven by an old Afghan who trudged along beside them with a long-handled whip similar to those used by bullock drivers.

We hurried on and reached the Louisa River just about sunset, but we were disheartened to find that it was in flood. This was most alarming, as we knew that this water, as well as the flood waters of the Margaret, was emptying into the Fitzroy. We had thought to be able to race the waters of the Margaret to the Fitzroy Crossing, but now, with the Louisa holding us up, our chances of crossing the Fitzroy looked very meagre. We were somewhat relieved to find that the water in the Louisa was falling, and therefore we hoped to be able to cross the following day. For the present there was nothing to do but camp, so we went back about a mile to a little rocky hill, as it would be very foolish to camp on low ground in the wet season. The sky was full of clouds, and, if rain fell that night, that rocky hill might be our home for months. Imagine then what an anxious night we passed! It did rain, too —a little—but not enough to do any harm.

Jack took off the rear mudguards and fitted double tyres on the back wheels (for which purpose we were carrying special attachments), as we knew that crossing the Louisa was going to be a tough proposition. We had been warned that the Louisa would be difficult to negotiate if we found it wet, as its sand is even more like quicksand than that of the others we had passed over, and they were bad enough.

CHAPTER SIXTEEN

So anxious were we that next morning we were up and had our breakfast over before the sun had properly risen. While I was packing up. Jack drove down to have a look at the river and came back with the joyful news that we would be able to cross.

We lost no time in putting on the load and getting down to the water's edge.

We had brought with us two "caterpillars" for the front wheels. Each "caterpillar" was made of two long pieces of heavy rope with slats of wood across—something like a flexible ladder. The rope fitted on each side of the wheel so that the tyre ran on the slats. Each "caterpillar" was made fast to the wheel with straps in such a way that it turned with it. We had brought these caterpillars" with us all the way from Brisbane—a distance of four thousand miles—and this was the first time we used them.

The Louisa River must be about 125 yards wide and. as we had no black boys to help us here, we ourselves had to carry the heavier part of the load across.

This meant many journeys backwards and forwards, and we realised how hard it was going to be for the car as our feet used to sink so far into the soft sand. There were two channels of water from a foot to eighteen inches deep—one channel running near each bank, and in between these two channels was a big bank of loose coarse sand.

While Jack was fitting the caterpillars" we were surprised to see a man on horseback driving a packhorse across from the opposite bank. The man we found was a bookmaker travelling to the Halls Creek races, which were to be held in about a week's time.

When one meets anyone in the bush the question "Where are you making for?" is always asked, and all the travellers we had met for hundreds of miles had given us the one answer, "The Halls Creek races." We could not understand why they were held at such a time of the year, when rain is so likely to fall, but we were told that that was the only time when people could attend. All the rest of the year, men are busy with the stock, but just before the rainy season everything is made ready for the "wet," work ceases, and the men are free to come hundreds of miles to the race meeting.

When they get back does not matter, as no work is done in the wet season. For some it is impossible to get borne at all until after the "wet," while with others it is a race with the fast-flooding rivers, men and horses often having to swim many of the streams.

The bookmaker we met that morning had hired, in Derby, a motor car which brought him out as far as Fitzroy Crossing, to which place there is a fair track from Derby. At Fitzroy Crossing the motor driver flatly refused to attempt to go any further, and the book-maker had no choice but to hire a couple of horses from a nearby station. He told us that, as he had not ridden for some years, he was having a very unpleasant journey.

With the usual kindliness of people in the outback, he waited to see if he could be of any assistance to us. Soon all was ready to tackle the crossing. The car, with its caterpillars on the front wheels and double tyres on the rear, reminded us of the tanks used in the war, as it came down the steep band and plunged into the first channel of water. She behaved like one too, as she came through the water and on to the sand bank before she stuck. We heaved a great sigh of relief, for now she was near enough to the far bank to be pulled out by our 75-yards of wire rope if everything else failed. However, we would only use that method as a last resource as it was so painfully slow and such strenuous work.

We dug the sand away from around the wheels, and with very little trouble, drove her across and into the other channel of water. Here in this awful "quicksand" she stuck fast, the sand closing in over the wheels and holding them tightly in its grip. We tried scraping the sand away, but that only made the car sink further. Using the engine, too, was useless, as it made the wheels dig in deeper and deeper, until our back wheels were buried up to the hubs in the sand.

Our only hope now was the wire rope. Jack fastened one end on to a large dead tree trunk (which looked very strong) and commenced operations, but so firmly was the car embedded in the sand that it pulled the tree trunk right over. Then he fastened the rope to a tree further up the bank, and, after a great deal of work (the bookmaker taking it in turns with Jack to use the winch), they got the car on to firm ground and Jack was able to drive it up the bank. No one can realise how glad we were to be over the Louisa River.

We had not stopped to have dinner, but, while the men were working, I boiled the billy and we had a belated meal.

We had no sooner sat down to lunch than the book-maker jumped up, gave a series of yells, and dashed down the bank of the river. Jack and I were puzzled at this strange behaviour until he came back and explained that his pack-horse was just about to roll in the water and the pack contained his roll of notes. His horse had been grazing nearby and had wandered down to the river.

By the time we loaded up and were ready to move off it was nearly four o'clock in the afternoon. We had spent nearly twelve hours in going about 125 yards.

We deeply appreciated the kindness of the traveller in doing what he could for us, as he would have to ride long hours to make up the time he had lost.

That day I was wearing a short-sleeved, low-necked tunic, and had my riding breeches rolled up above my knees. I got so badly sunburned that my arms, legs, and the back of my neck became a mass of blisters. For several nights I got very little sleep, and my clothes were a torment to me. I should have taken more care, but it was such a dull day that I did not realise how badly I was being burned. Jack, fortunately, was wearing an old pair of trousers, so that most of the time he did not bother having them rolled up. and his face and arms were so tanned that the sun could not make an impression on them.

We had a faintly marked team track to follow to the Fitzroy, and a couple of dry creeks on the way gave us no trouble at all. It is strange how the sand in the rivers in this district is made so much worse by the presence of water, whilst in most other places sand is much easier to drive over when wet.

Just as the sun was setting we reached the bank of the Fitzroy. Anxiety had been spurring us on, but our efforts were in vain, as we found the river was running and had about five feet of water in it, so of course, it was impossible for us to cross. On the other side of the Fitzroy River there were a few buildings—a hotel, a store run by the hotelkeeper, a police and a telegraph station—while on the side on which we were stranded there was nothing whatever.

I am afraid that I am unable to properly convey to you an impression of the Fitzroy River. It is an immense sandy bed several hundreds of yards wide with steep sandy banks. The water running in it was only about fifty yards wide, but it made one shudder to think what a mighty surging torrent that river would become when fully flooded. We were told later that the Fitzroy drains an area of something like fifty thousand square miles. The surrounding country is so flat that, in some places, the flood extends as far as sixty miles on either side of the river. There would be isolated dry patches here and there, but only an old hand would know where to find them.

We were also told that no car has ever crossed the Fitzroy under its own power, and it certainly looks as if no car will until something has been done to the crossing. All cars have had to be towed across by a donkey team kindly lent by the hotelkeeper, or by teams of blacks who attach ropes to the car and pull it across. We were soon seen by some blacks who told the policeman of our arrival, and next morning he came across on horseback to have a talk with us. He told us that it was the first fresh of the season, and the water had only started to rise on the morning of our arrival. The policeman said that probably the fresh would soon go down, and we might be able to cross the next morning. He promised to have a team of blacks ready to assist us across if the water were shallow enough.

After dark, in many places, but more especially here near the Fitzroy, we were annoyed by swarms of flying insects. The moment we switched on the lights they would come round in thousands and crawl all over us. Unfortunately, many of them were able to sting and, as some of them got in among our blankets, they annoyed us long after we turned out the lights.

Jack took advantage of the enforced delay to grease and inspect the car thoroughly, whilst every little while I kept running down the bank and sticking little pegs in at the water's edge to see if the river was rising or falling. It fell steadily until the middle of the afternoon, when it began to rise rapidly. Next morning we found the water a foot deeper than when we had arrived at the river. The policeman came across again and told us that there was very little hope of the water's falling again, as word had been received at the telegraph station of heavy rains around Hall's Creek and other areas which drain into the Fitzroy. He told us also that the place where we were camped was below flood level, so we would have to go back many miles on to high ground if we wanted to camp until the wet season was over. Where the buildings were, on the other side of the river, was just an island in time of flood. We could have got across to the hotel as the hotelkeeper had a boat, but we would have had to abandon our car, and that we were not prepared to do.

We were on the south side of the Fitzroy which runs from east to west. We saw by our map that, after crossing the river (supposing we were able to get across), we would have to travel down the north side for about two hundred miles on the track towards Derby, then cross the Fitzroy again at Yeeda Crossing, getting once more on the south side of the river in order to reach Broome, which is one hundred miles further on.

We asked the policeman if he thought it possible for us to get down the two hundred miles on the south side, and so avoid crossing the Fitzroy at all. He said that it would be an exceedingly difficult journey, as there was not even a bridle track to follow. No vehicle had ever been down that way and he considered that there was only a small chance of our getting through; but he said, if he were in our position, he would attempt it, as anything was better than remaining idle. He informed us that there was a station called Go-Go six miles down the river, and he thought the stockmen there might be able to give us some information about the country.

That morning the hotelkeeper sent a boy over with the boat to take us across to the store where we got some petrol that had been placed there for us. We also bought some food supplies, as we were very likely to be held up anywhere on that three hundred mile stretch ahead of us.

Early that afternoon we could see what looked like a heavy storm approaching. We thought it was going to rain about a foot, but it proved to be only a heavy wall of dust being swept on by cyclonic wind. We had the car almost packed ready to move on, so we threw the tarpaulin over the top, and, tying it down, sat underneath until the wind and dust had passed. Then we set out for Go-Go station, and by the time we reached there rain was just beginning to fall.

The bookkeeper made us welcome and presently, when the manager and a couple of the men came in, we discussed our plans. They all agreed that it seemed about the only thing left to do, but most of them thought that we were tackling an impossible task. They told us of a man who had tried to get down that way with some pack camels, but he had been forced to turn back because of the roughness of the country.

As there would be no track to follow—not even a bridle track — Mr. Millard, the manager, offered to lend us a black boy to act as guide. He lent us "Splinter," who, from what I understand, was his best station boy.

We are very grateful to Mr. Millard for this, as, but for his kindness, it is quite likely that I would not be here now to tell the tale.

He told us that, about 150 miles down the river, we would come to an outcamp where we would prob- ably be able to borrow another black boy, then we could let Splinter come home. "But how will he get back?" we both said at once. "Oh, he'll walk." Said Mr. Millard. That, evidently, was nothing to a black boy. Certainly he might meet wandering tribes, and, living with each for a few days, take his own time on the return journey.

The blacks are wonderful walkers. They have very thin legs, but they must be nearly all muscle. We heard of one boy who was sent with a letter to a station twenty-five miles away. He was one of the older black boys and, as he could not ride a horse, he had to walk.

The man to whom he gave the letter forgot to see that the boy was given food and, giving him the reply, sent him straight back again. The boy did the return journey, which means that he did fifty miles without food, although he was not a young man. We understand that the trip was done in one day which, I suppose, is not improbable, seeing the walkers' habits of life.

The blacks do not conserve food or make any provision for the morrow. When a blackfellow captures anything he usually makes a big meal and then camps until he is hungry. This means that he is nearly always hungry when he starts on the chase, and often goes for some time before his hunger is appeased. Of course, a blackfellow has such a wonderful knowledge of nature and the bush, that he is able to obtain both food and water where a white man would perish.

Go-Go is built almost on the bank of the Fitzroy on the highest bit of land that could be found around there. It is only just above flood level, and practically every year the flood waters come into the kitchen, so that for a few days the cook is paddling about in a foot or two of water. Before the floods come, most of the cattle are driven on to high land, and the few that are left may be fortunate enough to find small patches of dry land for themselves, but it often happens that many of the poor creatures are drowned.

CHAPTER SEVENTEEN

We were up earlv next morning and had our car well packed before daylight. After a hurried breakfast we got a good early start just as the day was breaking. We managed to find room for the black boy to sit up on top of the deck among the luggage. Splinter, who was somewhere about thirty, was a fine, tall, well-built black. Lending us such a boy was another example of Mr. Millard's thoughtfulness, as Splinter's physical strength was of great assistance to us that day.

For the first twelve miles the going was good. Only once were we bogged, and that time in the middle of a flat with no large tree near to which we could attach a wire rope. We spent some time putting small boughs under the wheels but had only been able to move the car a few inches. It looked as if we were in for a bad time when Splinter caught sight of four walk-about blacks and soon called them over to our assistance. Although they wore no clothes while on the walk-about, they were not "myalls" having probably worked for a while on a station at some time. They could speak only a few words of pidgin English, so Splinter soon explained in their own tongue what we wanted of them. With their help the car was soon out and they were rewarded with the usual presents of tobacco and red handkerchiefs. These were the last blacks we saw that day although, most likely, many saw us. We had been told at Go-Go that this country, especially the St. George Ranges which we were approaching, was infested with wild blacks but we would not see them as the "myall" takes good care of that.

Several times during the day we saw thin columns of smoke some distance away, but not before they had been pointed out to us by Splinter. These were from camp fires of the blacks who, very likely, were signalling to one another about our presence, as the blacks have a wonderful code for signalling by smoke. Messages sent in this way are said by the whites to have been sent by "mulga wire."

We were also told that we would have nothing to fear from even the wildest blacks while just passing through the country. They have not enough courage to attempt an open straight-forward attack, probably because they have heard of the punishment that almost invariably follows an attack on white men. However, you couldn't trust them too far. If you were camped some time among these wild blacks they would watch your movements, and, if they saw a chance of killing you without incurring any risk themselves, you would probably (as my husband expresses it) get a good view from the inside, or perhaps they might kill you to get your supplies and possessions.

The thought of the blacks did not worry us at all.

We had been assured that they would not attack us, we were well armed, we had Splinter with us, and somehow, not seeing any blacks gives one a sense of security.

Soon after getting out of the bog where the blacks assisted us, we came to Christmas Creek which we had been warned might give us trouble. Beyond that no-one seemed to be able to tell us much. Some of the men had ridden down that way a few miles and one man had gone down about thirty or forty miles. He it was who held out the least hope of our being able to get through. He told us how the St. George ranges extend right in to the bank of the river thus forcing a traveller to go in and out among the billabongs near the river bank. Billabongs are holes and channels at the side of the main river bed and it is because of these mountains and billabongs that traffic always goes along the north side of the river.

Christmas Creek, which had steep banks, was not very wide but it had been running recently and the bed of the creek was still wet. Jack tried to take it at a rush but the wheels just spun round when they got on to the soaked silty soil, and though Splinter and I pushed, the wheels just dug further in. The three of us then set to work and unloaded the car. carrying all the heavy goods up the far bank: then, after spending some minutes putting down branches, we managed to drive the car up the bank.

It was very hot weather and Jack and I were taking a drink about every twenty minutes but Splinter steadily refused a drink until nearly mid-day. Many of the white bushmen become, like the blacks, so used to the climate that they too can go without water for what would be to us an insufferably long period.

Soon after leaving Christmas Creek the St. George Ranges came into view. As there was no track whatever for us to follow, Splinter would pick out a particular mountain or large tree and tell us to go towards that. Often, when we came to the bank of a creek, we would spend some time looking for the best place to cross. As we got nearer the Ranges, the creeks and billabongs became far more numerous and more difficult to negotiate.

Splinter's knowledge of the country and his memory were nothing short of marvellous. He would point towards some trees and say, "Him big fella creek: no crossem that one there", and pointing either up or down the creek would say, "Might crossem that way".

Sure enough, we would find that Splinter always led us to what appeared to be the best place to cross. How he knew it. I cannot say, as there had never been a wheeled vehicle down there before.

Sometimes the far bank, or both banks, would be almost perpendicular everywhere we looked. Then the only thing we could do was to let the car down as gently as possible into the bed of the creek and haul her up the other side with the wire rope.

There were many heavy clouds about and we knew that, if it rained, we might become so badly bogged that it would be impossible to get the car out before the flood caught us. We knew we were below flood level all the time for about fifteen feet up in the branches of the trees we could see the debris from last year's flood. It was no wonder that we worked so strenuously as every moment counted.

I have since regretted the wonderful snapshots I missed that day but so great was our anxiety that the camera was never once thought of. Occasionally we would get on to a bit of a flat where we would be able to travel at a fair pace for a mile or two; but even then we were haunted by the fear of hitting an anthill, rock, or stump, in the long dry grass which in many places was higher than the hood. Most of the time, however, the ground surface was very troublesome. Sometimes we would have to go through sand which was so heavy that the car only managed to keep going in low gear even though Splinter and I would jump off and follow up behind.

We encountered miles and miles of spinifex flats which proved the roughest country Jack or I had ever seen. The soil was of a firm sandy nature covered with clumps of spinifex. For some weeks every year these flats are under several feet of fast-running water which washes the sandy soil away from in between the clumps of spinifex, and leaves them growing on little mounds of soil which has been held firmly by the roots. I can think of no way of describing it better than by saying it was like driving over inverted buckets of cement, each one set firmly and protruding a foot or eighteen inches above the level of the ground. It was a common thing to hear the body creaking and groaning because of two diagonal wheels being on top of two of these clumps while the other two wheels were practically swinging in the air. First gear was much too fast for such country and Jack had to keep slipping the clutch. Needless to say, I didn't attempt to take the wheel at all that day.

About mid-day we stopped for a few minutes to snatch a bite to eat and then it began to rain and rained steadily for about an hour. We were travelling with the hood down and so became wet to the skin as we couldn't afford to waste the time it would take to put up the hood which, in this case, would have been a lengthy process seeing that a number of things on the top, which were strapped on to the hood, would first have to be removed.

We were now skirting the foot of the St. George Ranges and that afternoon were nearly all the time pulling ourselves out of bogs or up the steep banks of billabongs. We would be driving along when, without any warning, the car would sink down until both axels would be resting in the mud and it often seemed as if only the running boards were preventing us from disappearing altogether. The wheels would just spin in the mud and, of course, the engine was useless, so it would be a case for the wire rope which we kept on the running board with one end attached to the dumb iron. Splinter was a wonderful help in working the winch and he and Jack would take it in turns as I was useless at the job. I insisted on trying it but found it so heavy that after a few turns my strength was gone.

When we would sink down into a bog-hole, mud would squelch up a few yards away so absolutely sodden was the country. As soon as the car was on firm ground we would get in and perhaps go only ten yards before we would be down again. When possible we put down boughs and Splinter and I pushed the car, but many of the bogs were too bad for these methods.

It was not the rain that had just fallen that was troubling us, but there had evidently been a number of storms within the last few days and the ground had become soaked to a great depth.

After being bogged a number of times, Jack decided to put on the double tyres which he had taken off at Fitzroy Crossing. Fitting them would take some time, but if they saved us from even one bog they would be worth-while, and so it proved, as, after they were on, we made much better progress. In many places there was a thin crust on the top of the bog and with such a wide spread of tyre surface we were able to ride over this crust without breaking through. Not that we weren't bogged at all with the double tyres, for even that contrivance couldn't save us every time.

Showing the Double Tyres Which Proved Such a Help in Mud and Sand.

We had luck with us as the following instances will show. We started off from Fitzroy Crossing with a tank full of petrol and two tins besides. Yeeda Crossing was approximately two hundred miles and Broome one hundred miles further on. making three hundred miles before we would be able to get fresh supplies. With all the first and second gear work we had to do, and the way we had to race our engine when bogged, we were naturally not getting a very big mileage to the gallon, and we realized the urgent necessity of husbanding our petrol stock. We felt that our lives depended on it, so imagine our horror when a tin that was on top of the deck fell off with a thud. We hastened to pick it up, hoping to save some of the petrol and how delighted we were to find that, although the tin was very much dented, it was not leaking at all. Some hours later I noticed that the tin which had been tied on the running board had disappeared. We sent Splinter back to look for it and anxiously waited for what seemed like an hour, although it was really only about ten minutes, then back came Splinter with the tin on his shoulder. It, too, was terribly dented and had lost its original shape, but, as in the first case, we had not lost a drop of petrol.

We were leaving the St. George Ranges behind us and the travelling was getting a little better when crash! we came to a dead stop and I heard Jack calling to me, "Good heavens, dear, what have I done?" It all happened in a flash. We had hit a stump in the long grass and the jar had thrown me forward against the wind-screen, breaking the screen and cutting my face. I have no recollection of hitting the screen but involuntarily I put my hands up to my face. The blood was gushing out between my fingers and Jack, of course, was terribly upset. He could not even see how much I was cut as my face was so covered with blond which was pouring out at a great rate.

The first thing was to stop the flow of blood as, if it continued to bleed like that, I would soon bleed to death. The nearest doctor was about two hundred miles away, so Jack had to get out our first aid case and do his best. He laid me on the ground with my head on one of the tarpaulins, and, on close examination, found that the cut which was bleeding so badly was a deep one just under the right eyebrow. He tried iodine and peroxide but they were useless as the blood gushing out soon washed anything away. Then he put his handkerchief over the cut and told me to hold it very still to allow the blood to clot.

Things looked pretty gloomy. The axle was bent in the middle nearly into a right angle and the sump was dented so that we thought the engine was damaged beyond immediate repair; I was hurt, we were stranded in a country inhabited by wild natives, and we were on ground that would soon be under fifteen feet of water. We ourselves could escape to the ranges where we might manage to dodge making a meal for the blacks but it looked as if the poor little car was doomed to be washed away.

I don't know how many times poor old Jack said, "My heart's broken!" and it certainly seemed to us to be the end of everything. Here it was that Splinter came to the rescue and told us that there was a station not far away on the other side of the river. This didn't seem much satisfaction at first, as a flooded river is a pretty effective barrier, but Jack decided to send Splinter across as they might be able to help us in some way. While I was holding the handkerchief to my face, Jack wrote a note to the manager explaining what had happened and asking for help. Splinter said that it would be just about dark by the time he got back. It looked as if the handkerchief was not going to be effective in stopping the bleeding as it became saturated almost immediately and the blood kept on trickling down the side of my head. Jack remembered having heard that flour will stop bleeding, although it is rather nasty stuff to get out of the cut afterwards. He took some little time to get the flour out from under the load, but at last came forward with a handful. When he took the handkerchief off he found that the bleeding had practically stopped, so it was not necessary to apply the flour. Instead he pressed on to the cut a good thick lump of cotton wool which, when the blood clotted, effectively stopped the bleeding.

I had been trying to persuade Jack to leave me alone and see if he could do anything to repair the car. Now that the bleeding had stopped I once more urged him to look to the car, but he refused to leave me whilst I was in such a state. He brought a dish of water and washed the blood from my face and hands, but getting it out of my hair was a hopeless task so that had to remain for the time being. After Jack had bandaged my face I felt so much better that I sat up. but had to lie down again almost immediately as sitting up made me feel so terribly ill.

Now Jack at last turned his attention to the car. The sump was so badly dented, as a result of the axles hitting it, that he was sure it must have come in contact with the crank shaft, but when he tried the engine he found that it was unaffected and started up quite easily. How relieved we were! Nothing else seemed to matter. Our car could easily be repaired, and we felt that we could now surmount any difficulty. Even although the axle was so badly bent, Jack, by altering the radius rods, was able to bring the front wheels sufficiently in line to make the car driveable. He put on the load and, by that time. I was able to sit up and get into the car, and soon we had it actually moving. It had a fearful wobble and. because of that, could only be driven very slowly in first gear. We started off in the direction Splinter had taken but we had only gone twenty yards when we were bogged. Jack investigated and found a way around that bit of a swamp so he quickly picked some branches which he put under the wheels and we backed out with very little trouble.

Darkness was fast closing in as we continued on our way once more, and we began to wonder if we had been wise in moving from where Splinter had left us, for he might come back with help and not be able to find us. However, we were not troubled long, for very soon we caught sight of several men coming towards us. They proved to be the manager and overseer of the station with Splinter and several other blacks. Never before had we been so pleased to see anyone, and. when they told us that the Fitzroy at this point was not flooded and that we would be able to cross, we were in the seventh heaven of delight.

Although we were astounded to hear that the flood waters had not travelled as far as this, they were not in the least surprised, and told us that sometimes the first fresh of the season did not reach their station, Noonkanbah, at all, but was entirely absorbed by the tremendous amount of sand in the upper reaches of the river. They were not aware that the river had started to rise, but, from what we told them of this fresh, they expected it soon to reach there.

With the assistance of the blacks we drove the car across the river to the far bank, but getting the car up this bank was going to be a tough proposition. The bank must have been about twenty feet high and so near to perpendicular that driving up it was impossible.

Mr. Williams (the manager of Noonkanbah station) suggested that we leave the car in the bed of the river while we go up to the homestead, a mile away, and have some tea; then they would bring down a donkey team and niggers and pull the car up the bank. Tea was ready when we got to the homestead. In fact, the men had been about to begin their meal when Splinter had arrived with the message. He had run all the way, arriving almost breathless, and, in addition to delivering the note, panted out an account of what had happened and finished up by saying: "White fella missus bin close up dead." The men couldn't make out what we were doing on the other side of the river, but they hastened to our rescue and told us that they were very much relieved when they saw us driving towards them.

We had driven seventy miles that day, and this we considered exceptionally good, seeing the condition of the country over which we had travelled and the difficulties we had encountered. Of course, we had started at half-past four in the morning and had been going at fever pace all the day.

CHAPTER EIGHTEEN

AFTER tea the men went down to the river to bring the car up to the homestead. They first unloaded the car and then it took a team of five donkeys, a score of blacks, three white men, and the engine pulling it hardest in first gear to get the car up that bank. If it had only been done in the daylight, what a photo it would have made! but the flood was coming down, so we dared not leave the car in the river bed until morning.

When they came back with the car I had to go through the ordeal of having my cuts properly dressed. Mr. Williams had a fine "First-Aid Outfit," and I really believe that it is due to the skilful manner in which he dressed my wounds that I now have only two neat scars instead of what I thought at first would be a disfigurement for life.

We all marvelled at my lucky escape, as the deep cut under the right eyebrow was so close to the eye. but had not damaged it. Had the cut been a quarter of an inch lower I would certainly have lost that eye. A cut on the bridge of the nose was not such a big one, but it has left the more conspicuous scar of the two. A few other cuts on my face and hands were little more than skin deep and so they have left no scars.

The cut under the right eyebrow was gaping and should have been stitched, but no doctor was handy. Mr. Williams saturated a piece of cotton wool with Friar's Balsalm and, putting that on the cut, bandaged it up. The saturated cotton wool dried and adhered to the flesh so that it kept the lips of the cut perfectly still, giving it a chance to heal. I was advised not to remove the cotton wool for many days, and when I did the cut was healing nicely.

That night of our arrival at Noonkanbah we felt as I think a captain must feel when he gets his ship out of a heavy storm into a harbour. Just a few hours before, our outlook had been so drear, and now we were here in a comfortable home surrounded by everything that kindness and hospitality could offer. We didn't seem to care if we were held up by the wet for a few months.

About nine o'clock the next morning word came up to the homestead that the fresh had reached the place where we had crossed the river.

Soon after breakfast we sent for Splinter, and gave him a note to take back to Mr. Millard. I told Splinter that he had been a good boy and that when I got to the "big fellow town" I would send him a present. Jack had given him a pipe and tobacco, but he had been such a help that I wanted to send him something else, so I asked him what he would like. He couldn't think of anything he wanted, so Jack, knowing how much use a bushman has for a pocket knife, asked him if he had a good one. He said that he had not, and evidently Jack had struck on the very thing that he wanted, for he seemed delighted at the prospect of getting one. Jack asked him what kind of a knife he would like and he said: "I bin like it plenty blade." We remembered this and when we reached Perth sent him one with four blades.

All that day Jack and Mr. Lukis (the assistant manager) worked on the car. They took off the front axle, and. by whacking it with a blacksmith's sledge-hammer. they managed to get it straight. It is evidently wonderful stuff that is used in motor car axles today, as this was the second time the axle had been bent, but it didn't seem to affect it, for, although we have done thousands of miles since, we are still using the same axle today.

I was feeling very weak as a result of the loss of so much blood, but that day's good rest refreshed me wonderfully. Much rain had fallen between Noonkanbah and Derby in the last fortnight, and storms were about every day. We would have to race the flood waters to Yeeda Crossing, and the water had a day's start of us, but this would be a small matter as long as we were not held up on the way.

After mid-day lunch the following day we resumed our journey. We carried with us never to be forgotten memories of the kindness of Mr.

Williams and Mr. Lukis.

Fifteen miles from the homestead was a creek which often gave a lot of trouble to travellers, and Mr. Williams insisted on accompanying us as far as that creek and bringing with him a couple of black boys in order to help us if we should get into difficulties. They came in an old Ford car which they had on the station. All the stations west of Fitzroy Crossing do their business through Derby, with the result that there is a fair bush track to that town. Where else but in the bush would one find a man go thirty miles because a couple of strangers might need a helping hand over a boggy creek?

As it happened, the creek was dry enough for us to get across without any trouble. Noonkanbah, I forgot to say, is a sheep station of one million acres. We found since entering Western Australia that nearly all the stations are that size, for there is some regulation in that state which prohibits more than a million acres being taken up in a single holding.

We noticed at Go-Go and Noonkanbah that "pindan" country was often spoken of, and we learned that it is the high red sandy country which is above flood level. It grows spinifex, coarse grass, and small trees, and provides food and shelter for the sheep when the low country is flooded. It is very similar to what is called "desert country" in the Northern Territory, only that the sandy soil of the "pindan" is loose and makes travelling very difficult, which is not the case with the hard red sandy soil of the "desert" in the Territory.

From Noonkanbah the track was only just dry enough to travel on, and we passed over many places which, two days previously, would have given us a very bad time. We drove until eleven o'clock that night, and we probably would not have stopped there, but we got a puncture, so I prepared our bunk on the ground while Jack was changing the tyre.

So anxious were we to make the most of the dry weather that we slept only a few hours and then we were up, had our breakfast, and were on the road again, while it was yet too dark to see without our headlights. Our car was behaving beautifully—none the worse for the bump we had given her, except that we had no wind-screen.

In various parts, but particularly throughout the Kimberley district, we saw many brolgas, or native companions as they are sometimes called. These harmless birds are tall and stately, being somewhere about four feet in height and of something the same build as a flamingo, only that the brolgas are dove grey in colour with touches of a bright pink on the head of the male.

We usually saw them in groups of from three to five and we enjoyed watching their dances which were at the same time graceful and ludicrous. They seemed to be dancing a regular measure, sometimes taking it in turns to perform and sometimes all dancing together.

Frequently they would look as though they were trying to execute some of the figures in eurythmics. We would often watch them for a while and then rush upon them suddenly with the car, for we enjoyed seeing them rise. Taking wing seemed quite an effort for them and was usually preceded by a kind of dancing run along the ground. They would generally fly only a short distance and land in a peculiar ungainly manner, keeping their balance by a dancing step before coming to a stand-still. These birds are protected now, but have become scarce in some districts, although we saw large numbers of them in the very remote parts. They were not very timid and would let us come fairly close to them in he car before becoming alarmed.

When within about twenty-five miles of Derby, instead of turning north and going into that town, as we had intended doing if we had had the time, we left the track and turned east to cross the Fitzroy.

We called in at Yeeda station, eight miles from the crossing, to borrow, if possible, a few blacks to help us over the river. The manager lent us an old black boy and his gin who were the only blacks available at the homestead at the time, the others having gone on a walkabout. He told us to send back the boy for a team of donkeys if we could not manage the crossing, but the donkeys would take some time to collect.

The river here is a tidal one but, luckily for us, the tide was out, and the water was only a few inches deep and a few yards wide, all the rest of the bed being an expanse of loose, coarse sand.

This place we had heard referred to as "Yeeda Crossing" but the word "crossing" is likely to mislead anyone not used to the back country. Somehow it implies cobblestones or a cemented way, but out in the bush it usually means just the place where the natural formation of the banks presents the least difficulty to the traveller. The banks here at Yeeda were low and of a gentler slope than those we had seen on any other part of the Fitzroy, so probably this place presents the only opportunity for many miles round for a vehicle to cross that mighty river.

We had broken our thermometer, so I do not know what the temperature of the day was, but it must have been about 112 degrees in the shade, and we were in the sun all the time. We fitted the twin tyres and caterpillars, then worked for a couple of hours getting the car across a few feet at a time. The sand was loose and seemingly bottomless, so the wheel would just spin and dig in, and we had to keep putting down sticks, stones and bags in order to give the wheels a grip. Then, when Jack got the car going in low gear, he would jump out and push and steer at the same time, while the blacks and I also pushed. We had to do this, for both the blacks were very old and of not much use.

I do not remember ever before doing such strenuous work, and by the time the car was across I felt just ready to drop, and fell down in the shade, exhausted. Shortly, I was seized with attacks of vomiting and thought that I must have received a touch of the sun.

Such did not prove to be the case for, after resting for an hour or so, I was much better. Probably the heat and strenuous work were too much for me after having lost so much blood a few days before.

We gave a tin of preserved fruit to the gin and black boy who helped us across the river. They were delighted and told us that it was "proper goodfella." I believe you could not give a blackfellow anything he would like better than tinned fruit. The fruit itself is a luxury probably never before tasted, and the blacks are very fond of sweet things.

CHAPTER NINETEEN

ON leaving the bank of the Fitzroy we steered west until we met the telegraph line and we made that our guide into Broome. It was with no small feeling of relief that we left the Fitzroy behind us and we felt there was nothing to stop us now. That feeling of security was only due to our ignorance of the country ahead of us as we were soon to discover.

Following the telegraph line was not easy work. We were travelling over fairly loose sand most of the way, and, with the heavy load we were carrying, we could only just manage to keep in top gear except when we struck very heavy patches of sand or sandhills. Although some of the sand looked very bad, we did not get bogged at all between Yeeda and Broome.

This part of the journey was a nightmare to me. Grasshoppers are my pet abomination—you know, those great creatures that are several inches long and have legs like young saws. This part of the country was infested with them and we were travelling without a wind-screen. What torture I suffered when those awful things used to fly in and use my face as a spring-board.

We had travelled only thirty miles from Yeeda Crossing when darkness came on, and that night we made a very comfortable bed in the sand. Travelling after dark was out of the question as we were driving all the time through long grass and over bushes and saplings. We were in constant fear of striking a stump, rock, or anthill, or of falling into a hole.

That night a very heavy storm fell in the direction of the track over which we had just passed and we could not help thinking how lucky we were. If the storm had fallen on that track the previous night we would never have reached the Yeeda Crossing in time, as, if we had been a half-day later in arriving at Yeeda, we would probably have found the flood waters there ahead of us.

Next morning we were up before daylight. We had seventy more miles to go to reach Broome, and, as it was Saturday, we wanted to reach there in time to get our mail. We thought the Post Office would close about mid-day and so for the first part of the day we hurried, but found that we were up against a hopeless task. so we gave up all hope of getting any letters before Monday. It was a pleasant surprise, therefore, to find, on arriving in the town about three o'clock, that the Post Office was open until six o'clock that night.

Between Yeeda and Broome we passed the largest bottle tree I have ever seen. These enormous trees have a large bottle-shaped trunk with leaves and branches sprouting out from the trunk, only at the top. This tree must have been about thirty feet in girth, and the trunk must have been about thirty feet high. The tree has a great heart of pith which, we have heard, holds a quantity of water which can be obtained by tapping. We chopped into this tree but we did not succeed in getting the water to flow, perhaps because we did not cut deeply enough.

For the last twenty-five miles before getting into Broome we were travelling over low-lying flats and dry mangrove swamps which would be rendered impassable by a heavy storm. It had rained recently, but the ground had dried up sufficiently to enable us to get through without being bogged, although several times had a few anxious moments, especially as very often there were no trees or bushes handy.

The town of Broome is built on a sandhill by the sea, and on one side of the town is a creek which gives shelter to many small pearling boats. The pearling industry really accounts for the existence of Broome, but, for the last few years, the pearlers have been having a bad time and many of them have failed and have been forced to give up work altogether.

A little metal is put up the centre of each street, otherwise vehicular traffic would be impossible. The sand from the sides of the streets blows over this metal and the consequence is that one cannot see where the metal ends. When we arrived in Broome we did not know this, and we had not been in the town five minutes before we tried to do a complete turn, and in a few seconds found our wheels spinning in the deep sand at the side of the road. There were many willing hands to help us back, and we had learned a lesson which we did not forget in a hurry.

There is a tremendous rise and fall in the tide at Broome, the difference between low and high water level varying from 18 to 28 feet. Ocean going steamers come in to the jetty on the high tide. They are then made fast to the jetty because at low tide they will be standing on the dry sand.

The population of Broome is very cosmopolitan. Europeans mostly own the pearling boats and do the dealing in pearls, while the stores are largely in the hands of the Japanese. There is only one white man on each pearling lugger, and he is the shell-opener. The diver is usually a Jap., and the crew consists mostly of Kopangers or Malays. In the town there is also a fair sprinkling of aborigines and various types of Asiatics.

One very interesting feature of the town was the Japanese cemetery. Each grave is marked by a slab of sandstone on which an inscription has been carved in Japanese. The slabs are brought from the beach where plenty of sandstone is to be obtained. You will notice that a number of bottles stand near the tomb stones. Some time ago, it was the custom to place on the grave bottles of spirits for the use of the departed. The spirits certainly disappeared, but—down the throats of the living, for men of other nations did not respect the customs of the Japanese. Nowadays, much to the disgust of the thirsty hoboes, only empty bottles decorate the graves.

We stayed three days in Broome—much longer than we had intended. The thought of those flats outside the town was worrying us. and we were anxious to push on, but Jack went out with one of the pearling vessels in order to secure some pictures of the pearling work, and so we were forced to remain the three days.

Such heavy clouds were hanging about every day that we were indeed glad when we could leave Broome behind us. For a few miles we went back by the way we had come into the town, until we struck a telegraph line running south, and this we followed. This stretch from Broome to Port Hedland, a distance of about four hundred miles, is known as "The Madman's Track,' because of the fact that so many travellers have died of thirst along that route.

It was delightful to be travelling south and to realise that with every mile we were drawing nearer to the region of winter rains where the wet season of the tropics was unknown. But we still had some hundreds of miles to go before we would be out of all danger of being held up by rain, and we could not be caught in a worse place than on these low-lying plains south of Broome, which we had heard were covered with several feet of water in the wet season.

Thirty miles out of Broome we came to a station where we were very pleased to accept Mr. and Mrs. Edgar's invitation to afternoon tea. They told us that rain was over-due and urged us to hurry if we wanted to get across the flats before the wet season. Mrs. Edgar was the first white woman we had seen on a station since leaving Moola Bulla, a distance of about 550 miles.

These plains, which extend for 250 miles along the coast, were wonderful to travel over in dry weather, as the ground was firm and smooth. Coarse grass and small bushes grew in places, but trees were very scarce and the few that managed to grow were very stunted.

Late in the afternoon a light shower of rain fell. It was not sufficient to do any harm, but caused us very now and then to skid and do a complete turn or two before we were able to get control of the car again. We could have prevented this skidding by putting chains on the wheels, but we did not want to spend the time to do this, and very soon we got beyond the light shower, so we were glad that we had not wasted the time.

We were afraid to camp on the flats lest a storm in the night might make it impossible for us to move the car. When at last, about ten o'clock, we came to a patch of sandy pindan country, we decided to camp there as that place would never become flooded and there was plenty of timber which we would need in the event of being held up for any length of time.

Before leaving Broome we had managed to procure some rain water with which to fill our tank and water-bag, as the bore water at Broome was far from palatable. Before going to bed I attempted to take a drink out of the water-bag, but found that the water had gone bad and was absolutely undrinkable. The water in the tank tasted good, so we came to the conclusion that the water in the bag must have been turned bad either by exposure to the air or by mud being thrown up on to the bag when we passed through the shower. We were rather inclined to the latter explanation as the mud on these flats certainly had an abominable smell.

On the Muddy Flats South of Broom e. Note the iron plates on the rear wheel for attaching the extra tyre.

CHAPTER TWENTY

ABOUT four o'clock in the morning we were roused by thunder and lightning, and we could see there was a tremendous storm right ahead of us. We knew there were more flats not many miles further on and that it would be possible to cross them, even if covered with water, providing we did so before it had time to soak in. We dressed quickly, bundled everything on to the car, and started off, but had not gone many miles when we came to the telegraph station at Lagrange Bay, just as the storm was becoming really heavy.

The kindly linesman, Mr. Connolly, had just been wakened by the storm, and was naturally very surprised to see visitors at such an early hour, but he invited us in and insisted that we stay and have some breakfast. By the time we had had something to eat it had stopped raining, as only about fifty points of rain fell here. We found there was a track across the flats to Anna Plains, a station about fifty miles away, and from there we would follow the telegraph line again.

We were leaving the telegraph line here at Lagrange Bay, and would not see it again until arriving at Anna Plains, as the telegraph line kept all the way on the pindan, which here was very loose sand, being part of the Great Sandy Desert.

After leaving the telegraph station we crossed a plain about four miles wide. The water here was several inches deep, but it had not had time to soak into the ground and we were able to cross then much more easily than we could have done a few hours later. After crossing this plain we found ourselves on the sandy pindan once again. This presented no difficulty as the sand was much improved by the rain.

After travelling seven or eight miles across the sand we came to another plain and here we could see water lying everywhere. We had been told that plain and pindan alternated all the way to Anna Plains, arms of the desert further inland being pushed out here and there to the very sea beach, which was only a couple of miles away on our right.

Evidently we had been on the edge of the storm at Lagrange Bay, as here many inches of rain must have fallen, for the water was lying a foot deep in many places. We must try, however, to push across that plain, as we could see on the horizon the line of trees that marked the next patch of pindan, and we hoped that beyond that we would get to country where the rain had not been so heavy. Owing to the amount of water, we could see no track, but we started off across the plain, trying to avoid the deepest water and the most boggy looking places. Before driving anywhere we would explore on foot to see if there was any possibility of getting through. Our shoes were useless, as they were soon pulled off by the heavy mud, so we had perforce to go barefooted. We must have walked miles and miles that day trying to find a way out. We were making for a little sandy patch where an arm of the desert had projected on to the plain without reaching the coast. About mid-day we found ourselves, after much hard work, on that little sandy patch, having done the two miles across that part of the plain in four hours.

After a hurried dinner, we started off again, and I shall never forget that afternoon. We were bogged times out of number. The only vegetation on the plains was a species of small bush which grew about a foot or eighteen inches high and was more like sea-weed than anything else. We must have picked cartloads of this at different times to poke under the wheels so that they could get a grip. Then Jack would rock the car backwards and forwards in first and reverse gear until she could pull herself out of the bog. Then, perhaps, he would drive only a few yards before he would be bogged again. Of course, I wasn't in the car at all. I spent all my time pushing the car or gathering bushes to put under the wheels.

It was fortunate that we had brought a large supply of petrol, as we must have used a tremendous amount that day. How that poor little car worked! We must have knocked her about more in that day than in weeks of ordinary travelling.

When within an hour of sunset we found that we had travelled only about a mile that afternoon, we decided to go back on to the patch of sand which, as I said before, was an arm of the inland desert. We very much regretted having to give up this mile, in the winning of which we had expended so much energy, but it would have been unwise to camp for the night in the bog.

These flats during the wet weather become really an inland sea several feet in depth. If we were camped on the flats, and it rained during the night, it might not be possible for us to get the car back to the higher sandy country. Getting back was not very difficult, as we had our wheel tracks to follow, and we got bogged only once.

Before turning in for the night (it was so like rain that we slept in the car) we bathed our feet which were very badly cut with the little sticks and stumps on which we had been treading in the mud. Then, when I had doctored up our feet with sticking plaster until they looked like very old much-patched tubes, they felt much better, although they were so sore that we could not wear shoes for several days.

Neither of us spoke a despondent word, and we both seemed to find quite a lot of things to laugh over and be thankful for. However, as we confessed to each other afterwards, it was just a bit of bluff with each of us to try to keep up the spirits of the other, for things looked blue indeed. We had failed to get across the flats and tomorrow they would be more boggy. It would take many days for the water to dry up, and before that could happen more rain would be sure to fall. We had been told that the flats were usually uncrossable for about four months of the year, and it looked as if that was the length of time we would be marooned on this arm of the desert.

That night it rained a little and our spirits really went down to zero, although we each assured the other that it wasn't going to be much, as the clouds weren't heavy enough. This proved to be the case, anyway, for the rain was too light to do any damage.

Next day we explored a bit. although our feet were too sore to do much walking. The water lying about was not quite so deep, but the ground was more boggy than ever. We knew it would be impossible to make any progress, so we just had to sit still and wait, hoping for a good hot sun and no rain. We got our wishes about the rain, although the sky was overcast all the day.

The following day we started off in a slightly different direction and managed to drive two miles by going around numerous swampy places. Then we discovered a worse swamp than we had yet encountered. The water was not very deep, but the mud was so soft and slushy' that we would sink half-way up to our knees when we tried to walk into it. It seemed to extend for miles, so we had to turn round and once more seek our sandy refuge.

We had been talking the previous day of trying to get to Anna Plains by following the telegraph line across the desert. At Lagrange Bay we had been told that it was impossible for us to travel along by the telegraph line owing to the heavy sand, but it is wonderful what one can do when necessity drives. We realised that waiting for the bog to dry up was useless, so the route across the desert was our only chance.

We knew that the telegraph line was somewhere on our left in among the stunted timber, and we set off to find it. I suggested that we go in slightly different directions, but Jack insisted on our keeping together owing to the possibility of my getting lost. We took a billy of water, biscuits, and a rifle, and we found the telegraph line nearer than we had expected, it being only about a mile away.

The rest of the afternoon we spent in shooting pigeons. We shot fifteen—enough to do us for tea, breakfast and dinner the following day. They were the little grey top-knot pigeons that seem to be found in almost every corner of Australia. These were a great change from tinned meat and we enjoyed them immensely.

I made a damper that night ready for the morrow's journey. Owing to the hospitality of the station people this was only the third damper I had had to make on the whole trip. The other two I had made while camped on the bank of the Fitzroy. Many times we had been without bread for several meals, but we had used dry biscuits in order to save the time it took to make a damper. As we were not carrying a camp oven, I made my dampers in a frying pan. This I would stand on some coals, and, when the damper (which was really a big scone the size of the pan) was cooked on one side, I would turn it over and allow it to cook on the other side.

We had long ere this run out of water, and we were drinking the water out of the bog. This water was so muddy that it was almost like soup (with apologies to the soup), and it is a wonder that it didn't make us ill. We thought of this possibility and boiled some, but the taste was then so abominable that we much preferred the muddy water which didn't taste bad at all. We found that the water which collected in our wheel tracks was not quite so muddy, so we went along and dipped enough out with a cup to fill all our billy-cans and dishes. To this we added a few grains of permanganate of potash and allowed it to settle all night. Certainly in the morning there was a good deal of sediment, but probably we did not add enough of the chemical as the water was still very muddy. This partially-cleared water was not enough to fill our water-bag, tank, and a small gallon tin which we were carrying, so we had to add some more of the dirty water to it, but the clarifying process certainly reduced the percentage of mud. As we knew that we had no chance of finding water in the desert, we had to carry as much as we possibly could.

CHAPTER TWENTY ONE

WE were up before daylight and lost no time in getting away, so delighted were we to be actually moving again. We had no track to follow, but the telegraph line acted as our guide. Part of the time we were driving over bushes and young saplings and the sand made the travelling very heavy indeed - although we had the twin tyres on the back wheels.

For 22 miles we did not touch top gear once, and the majority of that was very heavy pulling in low gear. We could not afford to waste any water by allowing the engine to boil (which, of course, was sure to happen under such strenuous conditions), so, whenever it showed signs of boiling, we would pull up and allow it to cool down again. Several times we were bogged in little muddy patches which extended from the flats inland.

Progress was very slow, and it was the middle of the afternoon before we sighted Anna Plains-—a sheep station. How glad we were to see a house once more. Mr. Hack, the manager of Anna Plains, greeted us with typical bush hospitality and immediately gave orders for after-noon tea. We stayed just long enough to partake of this, then set off again after having been considerately provided with some meat, hot bread, and a box of eggs. We hurried because we could see that a big storm was behind us and coming in our direction. So heavy it seemed that, I believe, if we had delayed our attempt to get along by the telegraph line for one day we would not have been able to get through, because of the narrow arms of the bog that stretched into the desert.

We were told where to leave the telegraph line in order to reach Nalgie, another sheep station about sixty miles away.

These sheep stations along this coast get all their supplies and mail by boat. The tide here has a tremendous rise and fall, as at Broome, and on the Ninety Mile Beach the tide goes out a distance of three miles. Luggers with supplies come in on the high tide and anchor. Then, when the tide has left them high and dry, the waggons are driven out alongside the boats and the supplies are taken off. With the next high tide the vessel can sail away.

After leaving Anna Plains that afternoon we ran into several light storms, but nothing heavy enough to trouble us, although we were on the same type of plain that had held us up some miles back. It was evident that the storm that had given us so much trouble had not extended as far as this, because very little rain had fallen here.

These plains were covered with roly-poly. This is a prickly bush which grows in the shape of a sphere anything up to three or four feet in diameter. When fully grown the plants break away at the root and the wind sweeps them across the plain. They look almost like living things bobbing about and running before the wind, and it certainly seems a very effective method of distributing seeds.

When darkness came we stopped and had something to eat. We knew that Nalgie must be very close, but we did not like arriving there so late and putting the hospitable folk to the trouble of preparing a special meal for us. Since leaving Anna Plains we had had the sea and a line of sandhills on our right and a perfectly treeless plain—almost desert—on our left, so we were unable to boil the billy for tea.

We were closer to Nalgie than we had thought, and very soon arrived there and found the owner and another gentleman holding the gate of the homestead paddock open for us. They had seen our headlights just before we had stopped for tea and could not understand what had kept us so long. They wanted to prepare a meal for us, but we explained that we had just had tea. Jack, however, was very grateful for the cup of tea that they insisted on making for him, as they knew we had been unable to make tea on the plain.

It seemed ages since we had been in a decent bed, as we had been through so much in the last few days. We were indeed grateful to Mr. Spry for his kind hospitality, more especially when, a few hours later, what they called a "North-west Cockeye" (really a fierce dry gale) came up.

The Sandy Desert near the Ninety Mile Beach.

Next day was Sunday and Mr. Spry suggested that we make a holiday of it and all spend the day "dry-pearling" on the Ninety Mile Beach. By "dry-pearling" is meant searching for pearl oysters that have been washed up on to the beach and into the shallow water. Sometimes valuable pearls can be discovered in this way, and we heard of one pearl worth £3000 being found like this on the Ninety Mile Beach. Most of the stations around here were originally taken up with that purpose in view. It was not then thought possible to run sheep on the desert. This was discovered later. How we would have liked to have accepted Mr. Spry's invitation to go "dry pearling," but we felt that, with rain hanging about as it was, we really must not spend the time, so once again we started out.

About sixteen miles from Nalgie we passed the telegraph station of Wallal and soon we found the flat hard plains give place to the sandy desert. We had thought the sand of the pindan loose and troublesome, but it was as nothing compared with the loose shifting sand we now encountered. Spinifex and a few coarse, very small shrubs were the only vegetation to be seen for many miles.

The further we went the heavier the sand became. Very often, when it became so bad that Jack would be forced to change down from second to low gear, I would jump off the car to relieve it of my weight, although The Sandy Desert Near the Ninety Mile Beach.

Jack used to laugh at me for imagining that my 7 stone 5 lbs. made much difference. I told him it was the last straw that broke the camel's back, and continued to jump off. I must have been very clumsy, as I would often go sprawling, but as it was always in loose soft sand, I never hurt myself.

There was a distinct track along here, made by camel and donkey teams, but they had churned the sand up so much that we made better progress by avoiding the track altogether.

We were trying to work our way through one very heavy patch of sand, gaining about six inches at a time, when Jack decided to put on the double tyres which we had removed soon after leaving Anna Plains. He fitted them right away, and they were a huge success, for the car simply walked out of that bad drift where we had been struggling for the last half-hour. We were travelling as closely as possible to the sandhills of the sea, as we had been told that the sand was even worse further inland.

Quite a number of sheep were running about here, and this surprised us very much for the country looked just useless desert. The sheep live on the bushes and spinifex which is practically always green and which, we were told, even a heavy dew will freshen. This country would indeed be worthless desert were it not for the fact that water can be obtained at such shallow depths. We passed many wells which were only eight or ten feet deep. The water in these wells was good water for stock, but, in our opinion, it had a perfectly vile taste. It was sweet, slightly brackish, and with a strong soda taste, some wells being much worse than others, and, in fact, the water of many of the wells was quite undrinkable. Although the water around here had such a horrible taste we had to keep on drinking a great amount of it, as it did not seem to satisfy one's thirst, and the weather was still very hot.

Although sheep are run on this part of the country, we learned later on that it requires about fifteen acres to carry one sheep, whereas much of the sheep country in Central Queensland runs a sheep to two acres. The wonder to us was that sheep could live there at all.

It was next day, when we thought ourselves across the worst of the sand, that we had our greatest trouble with it. We had lost sight of the waggon tracks for a while and presently we were bogged in a heavy sand-drift at the foot of a large sandhill. As we had come a long way into the sand-drift before getting bogged, it would have been a tremendous task to go back through that drift, and, even if we did manage to get back, we would probably have to climb some other sandhill.

We scouted round and discovered there was a gradual slope from the top of the hill in front of us, and that the country then appeared to be less sandy. We simply must get our car to the top of that hill! This would be no easy task, as the sand in the drift was that loose variety of sand which one finds on the ocean beach—in fact, we were almost on the ocean beach, and the roar of the surf could be heard all the time while, from the top of the sandhill, we could see the sea, which was only about half-a-mile away.

We tried putting down bushes, but the wheels spun round and quickly threw them out. After an hour's struggling along in this way we were disheartened to find that we had gained only ten yards. Then we came to the really steep part of the hill. Most motorists know how unpleasant sand can make itself on the level, but when one tries to climb a sandhill, from a standing start, where the sand is so loose that the wheels can do nothing but spin and dig in all the time, it is a hopeless task. We soon found that it was impossible to drive the car up such a hill. Had we been able to rush at it we might have had a chance of getting over it, or at any rate of driving some distance up the hill before being bogged.

We had gone for many miles without seeing any timber, but here there were a few stunted trees growing at intervals, and in one of these we beheld the solution of our difficulty. We could pull the car up with the wire rope, but it would be a very long process and very hard work. Fortunately, the ten yards we had gained with such difficulty had brought us to within easy reach of a tree.

To lighten the car Jack removed most of the load, then as I could be of no assistance in working the winch, I carried the load, bit by bit, up the hill while Jack was hauling up the car. Carrying the luggage proved to be very hard work, as sand is difficult to walk on at any time, and I had to make dozens of trips backwards and forwards. Jack insisted on taking up several of the heaviest articles, but I managed to carry the two cases of petrol by taking a tin at a time.

For hours Jack worked unceasingly at the winch, as we wanted to get over the hill before sunset. We had become bogged in the sand at the bottom of the hill at 10 o'clock in the morning, and, by working hard, we found ourselves on the top and ready to start off at half-past five that evening—just seven and a half hours to do seventy-five yards. We were so tired that we did not go much further that night, but camped at the very next water.

After that, although most of the travelling was very heavy and we were bogged a few times, we did not encounter any serious difficulties, and next morning, about eleven o'clock, we reached the station of Pardu, where we were invited to remain for dinner.

We learned at Pardu that we should have got on to the actual Ninety Mile Beach near Wallal, when the tide was going down, and driven as far as Pardu on the wet sand which is as firm as a rock. Had we done this we would have avoided the worst of the heavy sand. Between Pardu and Condon we crossed over a creek. Until we crossed this one we had not met with a single creek, or even a bit of a gutter, since leaving Broome, a distance of over 300 miles. The land is level, and the water soaks into the sand in the desert, while on the flats it just lies and forms a swamp until it either evaporates or soaks into the ground.

CHAPTER TWENTY TWO

FROM Pardu we followed the sea coast as far as Condon (a telegraph station). When we had started on the trip we had planned to keep close to the coast all the way to Perth, but at Broome we were told that we might strike trouble in the form of flooded rivers if we tried to follow the coast, and we were advised to go inland through Marble Bar and Meekatharra. We were also told there was rather a good track from Port Hedland to Perth via Marble Bar, but we did not want to waste time by going into Port Hedland, so from Condon we went south until we struck that track.

Soon after leaving Pardu we found that we had left the desert behind, and were travelling on firm, red sand, although for the next couple of hundred miles the main vegetation was spinifex and a few stunted trees.

We had been a bit anxious about the De Grey River, as it was possible that we might find it in flood. It was almost sunset when we arrived there and saw to our delight there was no sign of water at the crossing. It was a very big sandy river, but the sand was not of the same nature as that which we had found in the Kimberley Rivers, being much coarser and firmer. In addition to this, a double track of spinifex had been laid down right across the river, and so we went across without the least difficulty, not even having to change down into low gear.

We had tea before it got quite dark, and the track was so good that we intended driving on until we were tired. About eight o'clock we called in at a sheep station, Warralong, to ask the way. The manager was away from home, but Mr. Catling, who was in charge, would not hear of our going any further that night, and we were loth to partake of his hospitality. We learned here how close we were to being held up by the De Grey, as a fresh in the river had reached to within two miles of the crossing.

Although the track now was good, the landscape was rather uninteresting—one grows so tired of travelling mile after mile through spinifex. About twenty miles from Warralong the country became very hilly and stony, and around here we saw no sheep or cattle. Nothing but gold could bring men into such an arid waste.

Among these hills we came to Marble Bar, a little gold mining town with signs of having once been larger than it is today. We will always remember it for its excessive heat. Unfortunately, we had broken our thermometer, but in the Territory we had experienced a temperature of 129 degrees and quite enjoyed it. Here, in and around Marble Bar, the blazing sun and very strong scorching wind seemed ever so many degrees hotter. I do not even dare to make a guess as to what the temperature must have been here. We were told that Marble Bar is one of the hottest places in the world, and that it has an average maximum temperature of 117 degrees for the five summer months of the year. I never ascertained the truth of that statement, but one has only to pass through Marble Bar to believe it, and we must have been there on one of the hottest days of the year, which is quite likely, as it was the 21st December. Marble Bar gets its name from a big seam of marble which forms a bar across the creek about two miles out of the town.

The fact that we were travelling without a windscreen added much to our discomfort, and we suffered with cracked lips and parched skins. Our eyes, too, within the next few days, became very sore and bloodshot, for the track was good on the whole and we travelled such long hours at a fair speed.

About fifty miles from Marble Bar we turned out of our course to visit "The Lionel"—an asbestos mine. Unfortunately for us, work had ceased at the mine until after Christmas, but we were able to procure some fine specimens of asbestos in its raw state. We were surprised to find that it is a pale green rock looking in parts almost like opaque glass with a wonderful sheen. Strange to say, thin strips can be peeled off like bark off a tree, and these can be teased up until the asbestos looks like a mass of fine white silken threads.

We were in mountainous country for about eighty miles after

leaving Marble Bar, but we were no longer troubled by difficult creek and river crossings, as this country receives such a small rainfall —in fact, only about nine inches a year.

We were still trying to race against time, not because we were frightened of wet weather, as now we were well out of the area of tropical rains, but because we were eager to reach the town of Meekatharra for Christmas. We were anxious to have a rest on Christmas Day, and somehow we did not enjoy the prospect of opening a tin of bully beef for our Christmas dinner, so we rose before daylight each morning and drove as long as we possibly could, in order to reach the township by Christmas Eve.

I had discarded my bandage the day after leaving Marble Bar, as the cuts I had received from the windscreen had healed up nicely. The scars were very conspicuous, and for a while I was rather sensitive about them, but they gradually faded, and now they are not very noticeable.

For this part of the journey we were living on tinned food, and how we grew to hate it, especially after a slight attack of something like ptomaine poisoning. One day we opened a tin of tongues for dinner, and an hour or so afterwards we both felt ill at the same time. Of course we blamed the tongues, and, as we kept getting worse, we agreed that we must take an emetic. We had no mustard, so we took a drink of salty water, and in my case, this proved very efficient. Jack, however, drank a cupful and it only served to make him feel worse than ever. Whatever could I give him? I had heard that soap served the purpose, so I mixed him a "nice" drink of soapy water. He didn't like the idea of drinking it but I urged him to do it, and a few mouthfuls were sufficient—the emetic was a great success, and a very short time later we were able to continue our journey.

It was the day before Christmas Eve, and we were trying very hard to reach the little mining town of Peak Hill, seventy miles north of Meekatharra. We talked and sang to prevent ourselves from falling asleep at the wheel, but we had had many late nights like this and consequently, about eleven o clock we became too sleepy to drive any further—we just had to camp where we were. The ground was very stony, but it would take too long to make our bed up on the car, so we just threw down the ten flys and rugs and were asleep almost immediately.

Very soon ants began to crawl over us and bite us, then, while we were trying to decide whether it was worth while fixing up a bed in the car, it started to rain, and we had to grab our belongings and tumble into the car to get out of the wet. The rain was only a light drizzle, but it continued for some time. Other nights, when we had had time to make our bed in the car properly, it had been quite comfortable, but, huddled up as we were on this occasion, we spent a perfectly wretched night. Next morning, when we drove to the crest of the hill on which we had camped, we could see Peak Hill not more than half-a-mile away. To think that we had passed such a miserable night with a hotel and a comfortable bed so close!

We were still travelling over hard, red desert country, but a few stunted trees and a kind of desert grass were more common here than spinifex.

Meal-time in this region proved an ordeal. When food was placed on the ground it would become a moving mass of ants almost immediately. Where they came from and how they knew of the existence of the food is a mystery. The first ant to see it must have climbed up a blade of grass and whistled to his pals. It was a great comfort that the ants never came up on to the car. I do not know whether they disliked walking over the rubber tyres or whether they were simply unable to find a way.

CHAPTER TWENTY THREE

WE reached Meekatharra about mid-day on Christmas Eve and found the town full to overflowing. After all our hurry it looked as if we would have to go on and camp that night, but one of the hotel-keepers kindly went to a great deal of trouble and managed to make room for us.

How we appreciated that rest! So much did we enjoy it that we gave ourselves over two days holiday and did not move on again until the day after Boxing Day.

Meekatharra is a mining town a little over 500 miles from Perth. Our route from Meekatharra led us through several more little gold mining towns—Nannine, Cue, Mount Magnet and Payne's Find and we were able to make splendid progress as the tracks were dry and good.

As we went on, the nature of the country improved although it was still very sandy. We were impressed here by the quantity of salt that the ground appears to contain. Nearly every marsh, creek, or waterhole we passed had dried up leaving behind a layer of salt. Apparently, even when it rains, any surface water would be useless as it would become salty immediately. On the route we passed a fair number of wells, and water can be found at shallow depths. The water in some of the wells was good, while in others it was so salty as to be unfit for human consumption although it would probably be suitable for stock.

It was on this stage of the journey that we saw the largest goanna we have ever seen. It must have been about five feet long and it ran across the track in front of us. We were travelling very quickly, and by the time we stopped and went back it had disappeared, presumably down one of the many rabbit holes with which the ground here was honeycombed. These large goannas. we learnt, are a species of monitor and they are called "bung arras" by the blacks. In fact the blacks of some parts seem to call most goannas by that name.

We struck the railway line again at Wubin. Around here we were surprised to find large wheat fields with the wheat growing in light sandy soil—soil which we would have said was useless. In many places we saw wheat growing in what was almost pure sand. No grass worth speaking of grew in this sand—nothing but little furry bushes—but in spite of that fact the soil was capable of producing wonderful wheat.

In the Northern Territory and the northern part of Western Australia we had not seen a single rabbit, but in this wheat country rabbits abounded and were a great pest to the farmers.

All the way from here to Perth we were passing through wheat fields, and we heard that many farmers were growing wheat successfully on a rainfall of eleven inches per annum, simply because the rain always came at the right time of the year and it could be depended on.

It is only within the last few years that Western Australia has become a wheat-growing State, but now it is making wonderful progress in that direction. The harvest of 1900-1 yielded 774,653 bushels, while in the last harvest, 1926-27, something like 30,000.000 bushels of wheat were produced in that State.

We received a great welcome from the people of Perth. Everyone seemed to have a friendly word to say to us or good wishes to shower on us. We were taken to so many places and had so many entertainments arranged for us that it was a fortnight before we were able to tear ourselves away from the bright lights to face that dreary stretch across the Great Australian Bight.

We were to follow the Transcontinental Railway Line as far as Coolgardie, then go south through Norseman and Balladonia (a sheep station) until we met the telegraph line which runs along the coast, and this we were then to follow practically all the way to Port Augusta.

Perth is quite famous for its fruit, and just out of the town we passed many vineyards and orchards. Then we came once more to wheat fields, and through these we travelled for about 150 miles.

We were following the pipe main of that famous water scheme which supplies the town of Kalgoorlie. The Mundaring Weir is situated near Perth, and from there the water is taken a distance of 350 miles to

Kalgoorlie by a steel conduit thirty inches in internal diameter.

This wonderful water scheme has played an enormous part in the development of Western Australia. Gold was discovered in Coolgardie in 1892 and in Kalgoorlie the following year. People flocked there in thousands and cities grew up like mushrooms. Nature had endowed Kalgoorlie with gold, but had withheld that necessity to life water. The rainfall was a meagre nine inches a year, and all lakes or waterholes were salty that is, when they weren't dry. Tanks were almost unknown owing to the difficulty of transport in those early days before the coming of the "iron horse." It was useless putting down wells, as only salt water was obtained, so, in order to supply the town with water, salt water which was pumped out of the mines was distilled and sold to the people. Prices were exorbitant, and water was dearer than beer. A bath would cost as much as five shilling when you were lucky enough to be able to get one. The water from mines and wells was too pregnant with salt and other minerals to be used even for bathing, as it was so irritating to the skin.

It was at this stage that a courageous and far-sighted Government brought forward their wonderful "Goldfields Water Scheme" for taking water from the Helena River, eighteen miles from Perth, to the goldfields. This scheme was championed by Sir John Forrest and carried out by the engineering genius of Mr. C. Y. O'Connor. As is often the case with great works, much opposition was met with, but within five years the water was flowing into Kalgoorlie. Coolgardie has decayed and Kalgoorlie is not now as large as it once was, but the "Goldfields Water Scheme" has not been in vain.

Between Kalgoorlie and the coast a large number of agricultural towns owe their existence to the presence of the pipe main from which they draw their water. Although so many towns are already dependent on it, there is still room for expansion, for the present demand is 4,000,000 gallons a day and the scheme is capable of delivering nearly 6,000,000 gallons daily. This wonderful scheme has converted the desert into a garden, and as we travelled along by the pipe main we could not help but realise what such a scheme means to a country. Along the route eight pumping stations are situated, as the water has to be lifted a height of 1200 feet into the reservoir at Bullabulling, from whence it flows by gravity to Kalgoorlie, 44 miles further on. Large storage tanks of about $1^{1/4}$ million gallons capacity are also to be found at intervals along the pipe main in case of any accident happening to the conduit or pumping system, as the lives of so many are dependent on it.

About two hundred miles inland we noticed that we were leaving the wheat fields behind us, and as we travelled further east the land became more and more inhospitable, supporting only a kind of desert grass, a few shrubs and stunted trees. After all our trouble with rain it was wonderful to travel along with beautiful blue skies above us and to have people tell us that we could depend on fine weather, as it wouldn't rain for several months yet—this was the land of winter rains.

Even although we had been prepared for it. Coolgardie gave us a shock. Formerly a large flourishing city, it is now practically deserted, and the once fine buildings are a mass of crumbling bricks. When the mines failed and the population drifted away, all windows, doors, and sheets of iron were removed from the buildings, which, exposed thus to the elements, rapidly fell into decay. We passed many streets of buildings like this—structures that must have cost fortunes to build—and one could not help but feel depressed by this scene of ruin and desolation.

We found it still a large flourishing city, although it appears to have passed its zenith. We visited two of the mines in that world-famed "Golden Mile," from which £ 80,000,000 worth of gold has been taken —more than has been produced by any other square mile in the world.

Kalgoorlie is a city in a desert, but it is a desert only on account of its small rainfall, as the soil is wonderfully fertile. Water is plentiful now and cheap: in fact, the cheapness of the water is surprising. After being pumped uphill for the greater part of 350 miles, it is sold to private users for 2s. 6d. a thousand gallons and to the mines for 1/6 a thousand. Many folk here have beautiful gardens and fruit trees, and we visited one orchard where we were given some of the finest fruit we have ever tasted. If only science could bring a better to Kalgoorlie it would be small matter if the mines failed.

What a dry, desert-stricken place Kalgoorlie must have been before

before the coming of the water, and how hardy those prospectors who pushed out in search of gold into this waterless wilderness! What grave risks they ran, and how very many of them perished from thirst with a mocking mirage laughing at their impotence!

In Kalgoorlie we heard many tales of the old fossickers, of wonderful finds, and deeds done in the early days. I remember one story in particular about a man known as "Russian Jack" in the days of the Kimberley gold rush. With all his worldly possessions in a wheel-barrow, "Russian Jack" was tramping from Hall's Creek to Wyndham, when he came upon a man very illwith fever. The man was a stranger to him, but "Russian Jack" did not hesitate. Tipping out his belongings on to the roadside, he put the sick man on to his barrow, and, taking just enough food and water with him for the journey, wheeled him over rugged mountainous country into Wyndham, 140 miles away. This wonderful feat, I am pleased to say, was not in vain, for with care and attention the fever-stricken man recovered.

We paid a visit to Lake Perkolilli, twenty-five miles out of Kalgoorlie. For most of the year this lake is dry and its perfectly smooth clay surface makes a fine motor racing track. What wouldn't some of the large cities give to have it close at hand! The course as marked out is two-and-a-half miles around, but it could be made much longer if required. We raced around that track several times with the throttle wide open and wished that we could have some such track for the balance of the journey home.

CHAPTER TWENTY FOUR

AFTER three days in Kalgoorlie we made our way back to Coolgardie. then turned south, facing the wilderness once more, although we had several settlements to go through before actually leaving behind us the haunts of men.

About fifty miles from Coolgardie we came to a little settlement called Widgiemooltha. We heard here of a salt lake which was situated about six miles out of the town. We met the man who leased this lake, and he very kindly consented to go out there with us and show us around.

The lake proved to be a wonderful sight. The enormous expanse of dazzling white looked like a field of snow, and it actually hurt one's eyes to look at it, so great was the glare. When we walked out on to the lake we

Coolgardie.

found that we were walking on crystals of salt which were mixed with a very little water to the depth of about half-an-inch. Men raked the salt into heaps and later, when the water had drained from it, they put it into bags. In a few days' time salt could be raked up again from the same place, as a saturated solution of salt was continually oozing up out of the ground and the sun kept drying away the water, so that crystals of salt were deposited.

The lake—Lake Lefroy—was many square miles in area, but only a few acres were being used. Where the salt had not been touched it had set into a solid mass several inches in thickness, and so hard that to break it the first time a pick would have to be used. After it had been once broken the salt could be raked up frequently, as was being done in that portion of the lake which was being worked.

The quantity of salt that is here seems to be tremendous, as the glittering salt bed extended for miles and miles as far as the eye could reach. This little corner that was being worked was capable of delivering hundreds of tons per week. Imagine then what would be the output if the salt from the whole field were being harvested!

The production here was greatly simplified by the fact that the deposit was entirely free from impurities, and so the salt could be sent straight from the lake to the market. Crushing was the only treatment necessary to produce the various grades of salt.

That night we camped some miles beyond Widgiemooltha. and here, for the first time since leaving Brisbane, we had to keep a fire burning as a protection from the cold. Next morning we passed through Norseman and then had in front of us a stretch of eight hundred miles before we would strike another little township.

As we progressed east from Norseman the country became more drear and desert-like. This part of the country was suffering from a drought—I should call it a permanent drought with such a meagre rainfall. The weather was cold and an icy wind was blowing, the country was flat, and, as we could not seek shelter in the lee of a hill, we wondered how we were going to pass the night. Finally we chose a spot sheltered by some timber and brush, and. placing the car broadside on to the wind, built a windbreak (below) with all our suit cases, cases of petrol, and some bushes that we cut down. In this way we were sheltered to some extent, and much better off than we would have been in the open, but: we were still unable to get warm.

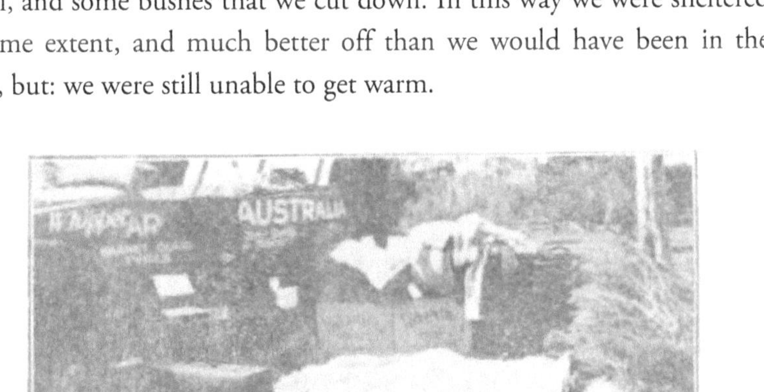

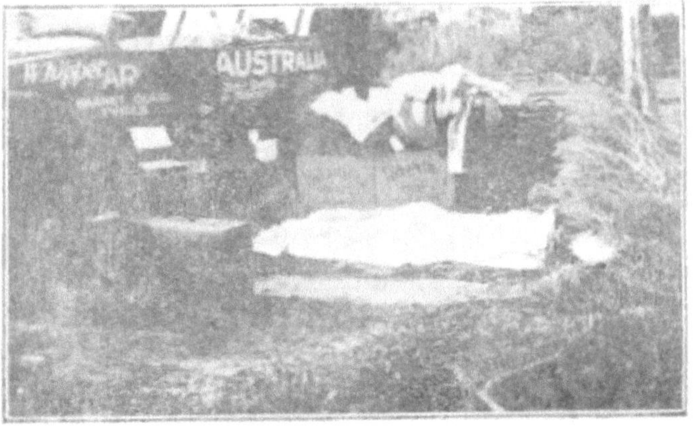

About mid-day the following day we arrived at Balladonia Station. Before leaving Norseman. 150 miles back, we had called at the Post Office and asked if we could take mail to any stations we would be passing. The postmaster was dubious about putting the two tremendous mail bags on our car, which was already overladen with the amount of petrol we were forced to carry. We, too, were somewhat dismayed when we saw the size of the bags, but we knew how much letters and papers are appreciated on those remote stations, and, when we heard that part of the mail was for a station, that received only four mails a year, we hadn't the heart to leave any of it behind.

When we arrived at Balladonia we felt very glad that we had taken the trouble to bring out the mail, especially when we discovered the hospitality of Mr. Poynton, the manager. We found there a beautiful stone homestead, much larger than is actually needed, but which has been built to enable him to give shelter to any tourists passing by. We were surprised to learn here of the kindly interest taken in travellers. Balladonia and Eucla are both on the telegraph line, so, when a tourist passes Balladonia, word is sent to Eucla 350 miles away, and, if the traveller does not arrive there in a reasonable time, it is taken for granted that some misfortune has befallen him and search parties start out from both places. We heard of several lives being saved in this way. In all probability this scheme can no longer be carried out as the telegraph station at Eucla was abandoned from 18th June, 1927.

As the rainfall is only about nine inches a year around Balladonia only a few stunted trees are to be found. Even the sheep-yards there are built of stone which is plentiful on the spot, whereas wood for building purposes would have to be brought from Albany some hundreds of miles away.

We left Balladonia after having dinner with these hospitable folk and then started off on what proved to be the most dreary and monotonous portion of the whole trip. The track was good most of the time, as we had neither sand nor rivers with which to contend, and there was no danger for we knew that if anything did happen to the car we would soon be rescued, whereas, in many parts where we had been, we could have been dead for weeks or months before anyone would know about it.

Soon after leaving Balladonia we struck the telegraph line which runs along the coast, and this line we followed practically all the way to Eucla.

No natural water is to be found in these parts, and, as it is limestone country, earth tanks would be useless for the ground would not hold water. Wells can be sunk, but to no advantage, as only salt water is, obtained. Men occasionally have to go along the telegraph line to inspect and repair it, so tanks have been erected by the Government at intervals along the route.

There are two styles of tanks. In some cases large sheds have been built with roofs of galvanised iron, and the water caught on these is drained into galvanised iron tanks. In other cases a very slight natural slope of the ground (the country is almost perfectly level) has been taken advantage of to form a catchment area and the water drains off into cement tanks built underground. There are two parts to each of these cement tanks—a small antechamber acting as a filter, and the large storage tank. In some of the cement tanks we found the water undrinkable owing to the presence of dead dingoes, rabbits, or birds.

It is wonderful how devoid of watercourses this country is. We crossed a small creek before reaching Norseman, and then we travelled a distance of at least seven hundred miles before crossing as much as a gutter again. Of course, the rainfall is only about seven or eight inches a year, so one could not expect much in the way of rivers.

Here and there we passed stunted trees, but mainly the vegetation was salt bush. This is a small bush somewhere about eighteen inches in height (although some species in other parts grow much larger) with a silvery sage green leaf and it forms good stock feed. It is very appropriately named as the plant actually does contain a fair amount of salt.

We were very uncomfortable during the first night after leaving Balladonia, as in spite of all our efforts, we could not manage to get warm. There was no shelter from the bitterly cold wind that blew incessantly. We slept on the ground, making use of all the rugs and the two tent flys, and even sleeping in our overcoats, but still we were cold. At last we managed to fall asleep, but only for a time, for about two o'clock in the morning we awoke shivering, and because of the intense cold we were unable to get to sleep again. We could not even make a big fire to keep ourselves warm as there was very little timber about, and that little was nothing more than twigs and sticks which would burn down in a few minutes. We suffered like this with the cold every night we were forced to camp out whilst travelling across the Great Australian Bight. The wind was so cold that all day long we would have to wear woollen clothes and our overcoats. We understand this is not always the case, for only a week or so previously the country had been visited by a heat wave and the temperature was well over 100 degrees for several days. I suppose we felt the cold more than we should have done usually, on account of our having just experienced several months of such very hot weather. We had a good track again all next day, but we still had to endure the same monotony of mile after mile of salt-bush plain.

At one of the wells we found an boy and a gin waiting for us. Word had been telegraphed from Norseman to Eyre Station that we were passing through and had the Eyre mail bag on board. The black boy told us that he had been waiting a day and a half seems rather a long time to wait for a mail bag, but it can be easily understood when one realises that Eyre Station receives mail only once every three months, except when some chance traveller drops it as we did.

Next day we passed three old blackfellows in a buggy drawn by two camels. This type of conveyance is used a great deal in these parts, especially by the men who repair the telegraph line. In fact, camels and motors are practically the only means of transport here, owing to the long stages between water.

Rabbits were very plentiful and the ground was honeycombed with their warrens. When I suggested that I should try to shoot some from the car, Jack laughingly told me that it was a waste of time, as I couldn't hit a tent from the inside. I was very gratified at my good fortune when my first three shots accounted for a rabbit apiece. Of course, Jack stopped the car to allow me to take aim.

We were surprised to see rabbits living in such dry country, but they must live on the salt bush, and, like guinea pigs, go entirely without water. Salt bush contains a certain amount of moisture, as we found when we crushed a handful of leaves that they made our fingers quite wet. Dingoes, too, were plentiful here. They of course have ample food in the form of rabbits and evidently the blood of these is sufficient liquid refreshment. I had always thought it impossible for a dog to live without water, but evidently these dingoes have adapted themselves to circumstances and climatic conditions.

Late in the afternoon we came to a line of very steep cliffs. These cliffs follow the coast of the Great Australian Bight for hundreds of miles, for the most part forming the actual shore, but, west of the point where we descended them, they leave the coast and run inland and parallel to the sea for probably a couple of hundred miles. We had been told of these and that we would have to descend them, but at the point where we encountered them this looked an impossibility, for the cliffs fell hundreds of feet to the plain below. This plain looked very beautiful in the afternoon sun, as, from the height where we were viewing the landscape, one would think that the plain (which extended as far as the eye could reach) was covered with fine grasses instead of salt bush, as we found afterwards to be the case. There were several eagles hovering around here, which seemed to be in keeping with the ruggedness of the scene.

The early pioneers evidently encountered great difficulty in finding a way down, for the track we were following ran along the top of the cliffs for several miles before at last turning down them. The pathway down was very rough and meandered a great way before at length arriving on the plain below.

A "Camel Buggy".

However, this is getting rather ahead of the story, for, when we had travelled some of the distance down the cliff, we came to a small flat shelf somewhat protected from the winds that never seem to cease in this part of the country, and here we decided to camp for the night. This proved a somewhat warmer camp than we had had on the previous two nights, but we were still far from comfortable.

During the night we were wakened by a thundering of hoofs, and Jack quickly turned his spotlight on to a mob of wild brumbies making their way down the cliff to obtain water from the bore at Madura Station on the plain below. This bore, by the way, is the only flowing bore within many hundreds of miles. Unfortunately, the water is only suitable for stock, being too salty for human consumption. When we turned the light on to the brumbies they galloped away in a great fright, but all the rest of the night we could hear them roaming around, and several times we switched on the light in order to frighten them. The track down the cliff followed a natural gorge, and seemingly was the path taken by the brumbies when coming for water. Evidently, they were unable to find any other way down the cliff, for when daylight came we could see them roaming restlessly about on the tableland above us.

Brumbies are wild horses—descendants of the ordinary domestic horses—but are usually such poor specimens, being inbred and undersized, that they are of little use. They are in fact, a great nuisance to the station people, for they entice the station horses away, and where these brumbies are present in large numbers they eat up the grass that in drought time becomes invaluable. On one station in the Northern Territory we passed the carcases of hundreds of horses, and heard at the homestead that the brumbies had become such a nuisance that 1300 had been shot. It was drought time and most of the pools for many miles round had dried up, so that the brumbies were easily shot as they came in to the little water that was left.

Before leaving camp that morning I made a large damper as we had run out of bread, and then we wended our way down the rough and boulder-strewn path on to the plain below.

All that day we drove along another plain of the same type as that over which we had been travelling on for the last two days, but the scenery was not now so monotonous, for we travelled most of the time with that line of cliffs close to us on our left.

We called in at Mundrabilla Station, but stayed only a few minutes. Some miles further on we stopped to talk to a number of blacks who were camped near a cement tank for the purpose of keeping some cattle supplied with water. This was done by lifting the water from a depth of from fifteen to twenty feet by the ancient and laborious method of lowering a bucket on the end of a rope and hauling it up by hand.

Presently we saw a number of gins coming towards us from the camp which was situated some little distance away. They were evidently actuated by curiosity and soon we found ourselves surrounded them.

A Beauty Parade Near Eucla.

CHAPTER TWENTY FIVE

LIGHT was closing in and Eucla was not in sight, we stopped and had some tea, and after that we had not been travelling long before we saw in the distance a light which denoted the proximity of Eucla. Often have I looked at that place on the map and imagined it to be a fair-sized town. When we arrived there the population was nine—six men and three women, but years ago about twenty operators and their wives and families were stationed there when Eucla was an important repeating station. Mr. Counsel (who was in charge at the time of our visit) and his wife made us very welcome, and how we enjoyed the luxury of a bed once again and a comfortable sleep sheltered from that freezing wind!

Next morning we took a walk down to the sea beach. Separating the buildings from the sea is an expanse of sand hills about half a mile across, and when one gets among these it is easy to imagine oneself on the Sahara Desert. These sand hills are continually shifting owing to the strong wind which is prevalent here. Before the building of the transcontinental railway all supplies had to be brought to Eucla by boat, and there is still a fine jetty standing. Running from a little goods-shed to the jetty is a trolley line, but this is now so covered over with sand that it is only visible here and there. Since the building of the transcontinental line, which passes about seventy miles inland from Eucla, supplies have been put off at a depot on the line and so the water route is no longer used.

The telegraph station and residences at Eucla were very fine stone buildings and it was quite pathetic to think that they were so soon to be deserted and Eucla was to be nothing but a name.

The telegraph line along the coast has always given a lot of trouble owing to its proximity to the sea, so a new one has been built following the transcontinental line, and on the 18th June, 1927, Eucla was abandoned and the other line brought into use. Judging by the way the sandhills are moving towards Eucla it looks as if it will not be long before those fine buildings will be buried beneath the sand.

We were so interested in looking over Eucla that it was nearly 11 before we bade farewell to our kind host and hostess. On leaving, we had to climb that line of cliffs we had descended about 115 miles back, but the ascent was quite easy as a fair track has been made up them to facilitate the bringing of supplies from the depot on the railway line. Ten miles from Eucla we came to a post and a cairn of stones which mark the border between West and South Australia.

We were following the telegraph line all the way and the road surface was good, but the wind was still blowing with even increased vigour and it was bitterly cold. It would have been a miserable night to camp out, but, fortunately for us, about 6 o'clock we reached the sheep station of Nullarbor where we enjoyed the kind hospitality of Mr. and Mrs. Brook. As we heard the wind roaring outside we felt very grateful for our comfortable bed and shelter. We learned here that this high wind is very common —in fact it is difficult to find a time when the wind is not blowing.

There are several bores on Nullarbor Station, but the water contains, besides other minerals, about $1^{1/2}$ ounces of salt to the gallon, so you can imagine how unpleasant it would be to drink, although stock do well on it.

Before we left Nullarbor Mr. Brook gave us a fine wombat skin. We had not seen any of these creatures although they are plentiful around here. We had passed many of the large holes that they make and wondered what they were, for they looked like rabbits' burrows only that they were very much larger. Mr. Brook was telling us the blacks are very fond of the flesh of the wombat, but they prefer to eat it in summer when the animal is unable to get water and is nice and fat.

Strange to say, in the winter time when the rain comes, the wombat loses its condition and the blacks do not like to eat it. We wasted no time on the way after leaving Nullarbor for we wanted to reach Fowlers Bay, 130 miles away, before nightfall. The wind was still blowing very fiercely and it was bitterly cold, so we wanted to avoid camping out.

About forty miles from Nullarbor we struck some heavy sand, and, though we did not get bogged, the pulling was very heavy for about five miles. It was a miserable bleak day. All the morning the sky was overcast and the sun did not appear until late in the afternoon. As the day wore on the wind seemed to gain in strength and we encountered several sand storms so thick that we could scarcely see two yards in front of the car. The wind was driving the clouds of sand along with such force that they stung and cut our faces, and if we had not had good closed-in goggles we would have found progress impossible.

As we drew nearer to Fowlers Bay the type of country began to improve and we came upon grasslands and wheatfields with homesteads dotted here and there. Just as the sun was setting we saw on the horizon before us what looked like a range of snow-clad mountains, but as we approached them we discovered they were huge hills of white sea-sand blown up by the wind and extending along the coast for many miles. They presented a most wonderful sight, eclipsing by far the sand-dunes we had admired so much at Eucla. About eight o'clock we arrived at

Fowlers Bay which is situated at the extreme end of those majestic ranges of sandhills.

We hoped to take some photographs of these hills the following morning, but it turned out such a dull, bleak day that photography was impossible.

That day we passed through Penong, and in the early afternoon arrived at Ceduna, where we were surprised to find a factory where plaster of paris is being manufactured from a deposit of gypsum not far from the town. From Ceduna we intended taking a short cut through the Yardea Sands to Port Augusta. This sand we had been told was very heavy indeed, but we had been through so much sand in the last few months that the thought of more did not deter us. We hesitated about leaving Ceduna that afternoon, as we would have to cover three hundred miles before reaching Port Augusta, the next township on our route. We dreaded the thought of camping out in the bitterly cold wind that was still blowing, but we were very anxious to proceed, and felt that we should not waste the few hours of daylight that were still left, so eventually we decided to leave Ceduna and endure the cold.

Next day we went through the Yardea Sands. The sand certainly was very deep, and it necessitated a good deal of heavy pulling and occasional labour with the spade, but it was not half as bad as some of the sand we had been forced to go through in other places. We learned afterwards that we had come through the Yardea Sands by the worst possible route, and we were told of three or four ways by which we could have avoided most of the sand.

The following evening we reached Port Augusta West and stayed there for the night, as the head of Spencer's Gulf, which is only a few hundred yards wide here, had to be crossed before reaching the town proper. We were much amused at the antiquated punt that conveyed us across to the town the following morning. It was made in the usual form of vehicular ferries with a flat deck and two sloping ends, but was towed on the end of a long rope by a small motor-boat. No provision was made in the form of a landing place and there were no posts to which the punt might be made fast. It was just pushed into shallow water where it was still free to float about. Of course, it would be quite a good idea if one could train one's car to jump on to it, but, as it was, when one attempted to drive on to the punt the front wheels of the car merely pushed it further into the water unless one knew how to treat this very erratic contrivance. There was a car in front of us which met with misfortune, for, when the front wheels were on the sloping end of the punt, it slid away and dropped the car into the water which was so deep that some of it got into the engine and temporarily stopped it.

We were given a good deal of advice as to the best method of procedure and we managed to get on board without any trouble. Then we discovered another unpleasant feature of this ferry. Queensland ferries usually charge one or two shillings, while in New South Wales they are all free, so imagine our surprise when we were charged ten shillings for being conveyed across that narrow channel of water. Now that ferry is no longer running, as a bridge has been built connecting Port Augusta and Port Augusta West.

The Punt at Port Augusta.

CHAPTER TWENTY SIX

SINCE leaving Brisbane we had looked upon Port Augusta as our goal, for now we would be travelling for the most part over made road and would no longer have to camp out, as hotels would be found at frequent intervals. It was just a joy ride from now on, and we did not hurry as we wanted to take things easily and see everything worth seeing.

Adelaide proved such a relief after that dreary journey across the Bight that we stayed a fortnight there enjoying the beauties of that garden city. A couple of days after leaving Adelaide we camped out again for one night while crossing the Coorong. This stretch of ninety miles included the roughest track that we met with between Adelaide and Brisbane, although for eleven miles of it, when we actually got on to the dry bed of the lake, the travelling was almost as good as on Lake Perkolilli.

In Mount Gambier we stayed for a couple of days and saw many of the scenic wonders of that exceedingly beautiful place. The beauty of Mount Gambier lies in its wonderful lakes which are situated in the craters of extinct volcanoes. There are a number of these lakes and a motor road winds around the edges of the craters, so that the lakes below, among forests of pines, form a picture that long remains in one's memory. We could easily have spent a week there, but home was beginning to call and we were anxious to be moving.

Whilst speaking of Mount Gambier, I must mention the wonderful building stone that is very abundant around there. It is white coraline limestone in which can be seen large numbers of shells—in fact, it seems to be formed of vast quantities of these pressed tightly together. It is taken out of the quarries and is so soft that it can be cut up into blocks with a cross-cut saw. Strange to say, exposure to the air hardens this stone and, with it, fine enduring buildings are erected at a very small cost.

Of the rest of the journey home there is very little more to tell. No more getting up before sunlight and preparing breakfast by a camp fire. No more getting bogged in mud or sand, carrying the luggage to hard ground, and then hauling the car out with the winch.

Good roads and easy stages mark the rest of the trip, and what a great amount of kindliness and friendliness we met with here in the towns and cities! From Mount Gambier to Melbourne the trip, though pleasant, was uneventful. When within a mile of the Melbourne Post Office we picked up a nail in a tyre that had been on one of the front wheels all the way from Brisbane without getting a puncture. We had been watching this tyre and wondering how far it would go before puncturing, and were even speculating on its chances of doing the whole round trip without a puncture. However, luck was against it, and it was hard luck for a tyre to cross Queensland, the Northern Territory, Western Australia, South Australia, and part of Victoria, over the worst possible tracks, carrying a tremendous load a distance of 8,500 miles, and then to be punctured by a nail on a beautiful bitumen road. As a matter of fact, the whole of our six tyres put up a wonderful performance as, up to Melbourne, we had had only three punctures, this one being the fourth. We had expected to have to buy a second set of tyres on the way, but not only did the one set go right around Australia, but when we finished the trip of 10,500 miles, they still were fit for several thousands of miles more.

From Melbourne we went through the famous old gold-mining town of Bendigo, then through fertile irrigation areas to Echuca on the Murray. From here we travelled down the well-known Goulburn Valley to Shepparton, and some miles further on, at Chiltern, Mr. J. Brann presented me with a young Whippet puppy six weeks old—a very appropriate mascot to take with us in the Whippet car that had served us so faithfully.

At Albury we visited the Hume Weir, which is in process of construction, then we passed through Wagga Wagga and Yass on to Canberra (our new Capital City). We then made our way, via Goulburn, to Sydney, where we began to feel really homesick, for Sydney was the last capital city, and we looked upon the journey from there to Brisbane as the last stage of our long trip.

From Sydney our route took us through Newcastle, Maitland, Singleton, Tamworth, Armidale and Glen Innes. This part of the journey was very enjoyable as the roads were good, the weather was perfect, and the scenery was beautiful. The drive from Glen Innes to Grafton, a distance of 110 miles, presented some of the most glorious views we had seen on the whole trip. We were getting more homesick with every mile that brought us nearer to Brisbane, our home town, and it seemed as if we would never reach there. From Grafton through Casino, Lismore, Mullumbimby and Murwillumbah was a delightful journey and we were much impressed by the beauty and fertility of this wonderful district known as the Northern Rivers. The enthusiastic way in which we were welcomed in the various towns forms one of the most pleasant recollections of the trip.

At last, on the 25th March, 1927, we reached Tweed Heads, where we crossed the border into Queensland. Word of our expected arrival had been sent on ahead and a great crowd was waiting to meet us. Here amid the cheers and words of welcome I had great difficulty in keeping back the tears of joy. We had certainly had a delightful trip and had been treated in the most wonderful manner by the people we had met on the whole journey. We had enjoyed our holiday immensely but we were longing to see once again the friends who had waved us farewell so many months before.

We stayed at Southport that night, and early next morning set out on the journey home. At Beenleigh, twenty-four miles from Brisbane, we were met by friends and relations who had driven down to greet us. Another large army of cars was waiting for us at Eight Mile Plains, and accompanied by these, we entered Brisbane, arriving at the General Post Office at mid-day. Judging by the welcomes we had received in other towns we thought that a fair number of people, including many friends and relations, would be present to welcome us in Brisbane, but we were certainly not prepared for the immense throng that greeted us, and the great interest that was shown in the trip.

Now we look back on our experiences and often long for another taste of the free, open life of the outback. The Northern Territory and the northern part of Western Australia, although by far the most difficult portions of the trip, are just teeming with interest, and we hope that some day we will be able to visit once again the friends we made on our honeymoon tour.

The Journey's End, Back at the G.P.O. Brisbane

The following list of the approximate distances between the various places may prove useful to others who may choose that ideal holiday—a trip around Australia

Brisbane to Morven	427 miles
Morven to Longreach	360 ..
Longreach to Maxwelton	300 ..
Maxwelton o Cloncurry	180 ..
Cloncurry to Mt. Isa	145 ..
Mt Isa to Camooweal	130 ..
Camooweal to Avon Downs	45 ..
Avon Downs to Alexandria	95 ..
Alexandria to Brunette Downs	65 ..
Brunette Downs to Anthony's Lagoon	60 ..
Anthony's Lagoon to Newcastle Waters	180 ..
Newcastle Waters to Daly Waters	90 ..
Daly Waters to Mataranka	110 ..
Mataranka to Marranboy	50 ..
Marranbuy to Katherine	45 ..
Katherine to Darwin	220 ..
Katherine to Victoria River Downs	200 ..
Victoria River Downs to Wave Hill	100 ..
Wave Hill to Inverway	140 ..
Inverway to Flora Valley	180 ..
Flora Valley to Hall's Creek	33 ..
Hall's Creek to Moola Bulla	25 ..
Moola Bulla to Margaret Station	70 ..
Margaret Station to Fitzroy Crossing	125 ..
Fitzroy Crossing to Noonkanbah	70 ..
Noonkanbah to Yeeda Crossing	135 ..
Yeeda Crossing to Broome	110 ..
Broome to Lagrange Bay	90 ..
Lagrange Bay to Wallal	130 ..
Wallal to Condon	100 ..
Condon to Marble Bar	105 ..
Marble Bar to Meekatharra	490 ..
Meekatharra to Perth	520 ..
Perth to Coolgardie	360 ..
Coolgardie to Kalgoorlie	25 ..
Coolgardie to Norseman	120 ..
Norseman to Balladonia	150 ..
Balladonia to Eucla	330 ..
Eucla to Fowler's Bay	260 ..
Fowler's Bay to Port Augusta	380 ..
Port Augusta to Adelaide	225 ..
Adelaide to Mt. Gambier	300 ..
Moun. Gambier to Melbourune	350 ..
Melbourne to Echuca	165 ..
Echuca to Albury	175 ..
Albury to Wagga Wagga	100 ..
Wagga Wagga to Canberra	160 ..
Canberra to Sydney	225 ..
Sydney to Newcastle	160 ..
Newcastle to Tamworth	185 ..
Tamworth to Armidale	75 ..
Armidale to Glen Innes	61 ..
Glen Innes to Grafton	110 ..
Grafton to Lismore	110 ..
Lismore to Tweed Heads	100 ..
Tweed Heads to Brisbane	68 ..

BARNET GLASS TYRES

www.ingramcontent.com/pod-product-compliance
Ingram Content Group Australia Pty Ltd
76 Discovery Rd, Dandenong South VIC 3175, AU
AUHW020942270526
427798AU00002B/26